Young People
and Death

Young People and Death

Edited by
John D. Morgan, PhD

The Charles Press, Publishers
Philadelphia

The Charles Press, Publishers
Post Office Box 15715
Philadelphia, PA 19103

Library of Congress Cataloging-in-Publication Data

Young people and death / edited by John D. Morgan.
    p. cm.
   Includes bibliographical references.
   ISBN 0-914783-49-1
   1. Children and death. 2. Bereavement in children.
3. Terminally ill children—Psychology. 4. Death—
Study and teaching (Elementary). 5. Children—Counseling
of. I. Morgan, John D., 1933- .
BF723.D3Y68   1991
15.9'37'083—dc20   90-28402
                                                  CIP

Printed in the United States of America

ISBN 0-914783-49-1

Manuscript edited by Lauren Meltzer
Typeset by Camden Type 'n Graphics
Printed and bound by Versa Press

Contributors

Rev. Beatrice M.A. Ash, MDiv
Windsor, Ontario, Canada

Myra Bluebond-Langner, PhD
Associate Professor of Anthropology, Rutgers University,
Camden, New Jersey

Kathleen A. Braza, MA
Bereavement Coordinator, Holy Cross Hospital,
Salt Lake City, Utah

Sandor B. Brent, PhD
Associate Professor of Psychology, Wayne State University,
Detroit, Michigan

Carol Chapin, BSN, MA
Bereavement Counselor, Office of the Medical Investigator,
State of New Mexico; University of New Mexico School of
Medicine, Albuquerque, New Mexico

Gerry R. Cox, PhD
Professor of Sociology, Fort Hays State University, Hays, Kansas

Thomas Frantz, PhD
Associate Professor of Counseling and Educational Psychology,
State University of New York, Buffalo, New York

Nan Giblin, PhD
Associate Professor, Department of Counselor Education,
Northeastern Illinois University, Chicago, Illinois

Rick Kelly, CCW
Mental Health Consultant, The Hospital for Sick Children, Toronto, Ontario, Canada

Sandra Kesselman Hardy, MSW, CSW
Consultant, Bereaved Families of Ontario—Ottawa-Carleton, Ottawa, Ontario, Canada

Dorothy J. Landis, MSW, ACSW
Social Worker, St. Paul, Minnesota

Corinne Masur, PsyD
Child Psychologist, Philadelphia, Pennsylvania

Brian McGarry
Funeral Director, Hulse & Playfair Funeral Homes, Ottawa, Ontario, Canada

John D. Morgan, PhD
Professor of Philosophy; Coordinator of Death Education Conferences, King's College, London, Ontario, Canada

Philip J. Mueller, PhD
Principal, King's College, London, Ontario, Canada

Sr. Caroline O'Connor, CSJ
Chaplain, St. Joseph's Hospital, Windsor, Ontario, Canada

Donna O'Toole, MA
Clinical Psychologist, Rainbow Connection, Burnsville, North Carolina

Richard A. Pacholski, PhD
Professor of English, Millikin University, Decatur, Illinois

Sr. Frances Ryan, DC, PhD
Associate Professor of Psychology, DePaul University, Chicago, Illinois

Rev. Dennis E. Saylor, PhD

Chaplain, Sharp Health Care, San Diego, California

Darcie Sims

Grief Management Specialist, Slidell, Louisiana

Mark W. Speece, PhD

Associate Professor, Department of Internal Medicine, Wayne State University, Detroit, Michigan

Wendy Wainwright

Hospice Counselor, Hospice Victoria, Victoria, British Columbia, Canada

Contents

Preface

In spare moments over the last weeks, I have tried to think of remarks that might set a tone for the reflections you might have as you read this book. I soon realized that such remarks presuppose a wisdom which I simply do not possess; although Plato would consider my age appropriate for wisdom, I have not thought much about death generally, and very little about my own death specifically. The problems that preoccupy me lack the existential poignancy of helping dying and bereaved people, their families and friends. In my work, people may occasionally emit a gasp in my office—they do not, however, tend to expire there. One personal experience which took place 20 years ago is, on the other hand, a situation which many people experience. The night my father died, I sat with him in a small hospital for about an hour. He spoke only a few times during that hour and I can't remember any of his words. What I do remember is holding his hand the entire time. The bond between us seemed more vibrant and stronger than ever before; we were at peace. At about 9:30 P.M., a nurse reminded me that visiting hours were long over. That night, after I had left the hospital, my father died in his sleep.

Years after the death of my father I read Tolstoy's *The Death of Ivan Ilych*. I was struck by the account of Gerasim, a peasant boy, who was the only person who refused to pretend that Ivan Ilych was not dying when he was with his dying friend and who alone provided practical help, such as propping up his legs to provide some comfort. When Ivan laments being a burden, Gerasim says: "We shall all of us die, so why should I grudge a little trouble?" Gerasim did not find his work burdensome, because as Tolstoy adds, "he was doing it for a dying man and hoped someone would do the same for him when his time came." I think we all hope that someone—preferably someone we love—will be with us when we die.

My belief about grieving is that as social beings we should be supportive of each other, especially when we come up against a "limit-situation" that reinforces that frightening but factual aspect of life—its finitude. Death is, beyond any doubt, the decisive "limit-situation." For the sake decency, we cannot abandon a dying or grieving person, but must, like Gerasim, provide help and support. An anthology such as the present one draws our attention to the need to be with the young and old as they die, and with the survivors who grieve.

In addition to this, I want to voice my appreciation to all those who serve and minister to the dying and bereaved. Your daily work humanizes a difficult and confusing life circumstance; you are with individuals in very practical ways during difficult times. By this you provide a marvelous example, a paradigm for being with others in a supportive way. Judeo-Christians see in this circumstance a reflection of *hesed*—the gracious, loving-kindness of Jahweh toward all humanity. We are indebted to you for such a forceful reminder that nudges all of us toward greater compassion and humanity.

On behalf of the many who are not involved in giving care to the dying and bereaved, I am pleased to voice this appreciation, together with my certainty that you, too, will benefit greatly from this book.

PHILIP J. MUELLER, PhD

Introduction

This volume represents the second in a series of texts co-published by The Charles Press, Philadelphia, and King's College, London, Ontario, Canada. King's College has been a leader in the study of death and bereavement since 1975, and The Charles Press has developed a wide range of books dealing with similar subjects. The present volume follows the publication of *Children and Death* (1986), *Suicide* (1987), *Bereavement* (1988), *Separation and Divorce* (1988), *Thanatology: A Liberal Arts Approach* (1989), and *The Dying and the Bereaved Teenager* (1990). We at King's College appreciate the efforts of The Charles Press in making our work available to a larger audience.

Several good books have been published on the subject of children and death. The information provided in this volume, however, transcends the traditional approach by giving practical advice and guidelines that caregivers—teachers, counselors, nurses, social workers, and the clergy—can use in their daily work with young people in this critical period of their lives.

We tend to assume that the life of a child consists of little more than the gathering of memories that in later years can be recalled fondly. In reality, nothing could be further from the truth. Childhood is, and always has been, a time of trial and loss. While not as many children today see a parent or sibling die as did children in the past, they do live in a world threatened by disintegration: nuclear war, urban violence, family breakups, drugs and AIDS, as well as the slower but inevitable disintegration of our environment. We hope that the information presented in this book will be useful to caregivers who help children while they mature and aid them in their need to integrate loss—as well as threatened loss—into their lives.

This book is divided into five sections: the first covers the child's understanding of death; the second concerns the care of the dying child; the third deals with the bereaved child and the fourth with the bereaved family; finally, the fifth section provides information on the role of the school. It also will aid schools in assisting unaffected children to accept and understand the significance of life and death.

The first section begins with an important contribution by Nan Giblin and Frances Ryan. Drs. Giblin and Ryan developed a sentence completion test to discover the child's perception of death. This test, in conjunction with photographic book and play therapy, provides the teacher, counselor, or nurse with the tools to help young children express their awareness of death as well as the specific issues they may be troubled by in the case of a particular death. In their chapter, Drs. Brent and Speece continue to develop their long-standing contributions to the supposedly "adult" concept of irreversibility.

The second section deals with the care of seriously ill and dying children. Dorothy Landis explains the difficulties of caring for children of a different culture and provides us with excellent, practical guidelines for doing so. The problem of care for children of different cultures will become more important as North America becomes more of a mosaic and less of a melting pot. Dr. Myra Bluebond-Langner, winner of the 1989 Margaret Mead Award of the American Anthropology Association, continues her work by developing a thesis about children with cystic fibrosis and the difficulties that families have in the care of seriously ill children. Thomas Frantz and Rick Kelly complete this section with superb help for caregivers who spend their energies helping dying and bereaved children and their families.

Caroline O'Connor begins a more personal section dealing with bereaved children by recalling the way she and her brothers and sisters were excluded from grieving when one of her brothers died. From this concrete example of the problems bereaved children have, we move to Kathleen Braza's chapter dealing with support groups for children in a hospital. Ms. Braza ends with practical suggestions for establishing such a program. Wendy Wainwright discusses groups for bereaved families in a hospice setting. Corinne Masur's work with bereaved children includes individual treatment. Her chapter is particularly helpful for suggestions about taking the child's history and presenting problems. This section on the bereaved child closes with Brian McGarry's discussion of the help that a funeral director can provide for bereaved children.

Section four, which deals with the bereaved family, begins with Sandra Kesselman Hardy's reminder that where death is concerned, we are all children. Beatrice Ash provides material indicating the need for grief work and the help that a clergyperson can provide in facilitating that work. The bereavement protocols established by the Office of the Medical Investigator in Albuquerque, New Mexico, are discussed by Carol Chapin in her chapter on sudden death and crisis intervention. This innovative program could one day serve as a model for government agencies across North America.

Gerry Cox's chapter teaches us that while the death of a loved one is painful, it helps us to appreciate that time is important and that life is lived to the fullest when relationships are cherished. This theme was considered earlier in Thomas Frantz's chapter on care for the caregiver. Finally, Dennis Saylor describes the different bereavement methods four men used to help them cope when their children died. Because so little has been written about male grief patterns, this contribution is a welcome one.

Schools are becoming more conscious of their important role in the development of children's knowledge of and attitudes about death. As Rabbi Earl Grollman never tires of saying, the question is not *if* we are going to provide death education—we do that by our actions and often by our silence. The question is whether the education about death and bereavement that we do provide will be helpful.

Donna O'Toole begins the final section—the role of the school in death education—with an examination of storytelling as a form of grief therapy. Darcie Sims discusses a bereavement model for public schools, and Richard Pacholski concludes the section with a chapter addressing the critics of death education.

It is our hope that *Young People and Death* will make a useful contribution to the work of educators and involved caregivers in all settings.

JOHN D. MORGAN, PHD

Young People
and Death

I

The Child's Understanding of Death

1

Reaching the Child's Perception of Death

Nan Giblin, PhD and Frances Ryan, DC, PhD

The most common mistake that adults make when associating with children who are grieving is to assume that children think like adults. In doing so, grieving adults frequently project their own fears and perceptions of death onto the children with whom they are dealing. The effect of this type of projection is that children miss an opportunity to learn to face loss in a manner appropriate to their developmental age, if not missing the opportunity to confront the loss altogether. Adults miss the chance to look into the fascinating and creative minds of children, missing, perhaps, a chance to view life from a child's usually unjaded point of view and consequently missing what could prove to be important methods for adults in coping with loss and death.

A good deal has been written on how children view death (Gesell 1941; Wolfelt 1983). Based on these writings, the following results regarding children's perceptions of death are given:

CHILDREN'S PERCEPTIONS OF DEATH

1–3 Years:
- Very little or no understanding of the idea of death.

4 Years:
- Very limited concept of death.
- Uses the word with some vague notion of its meaning.
- No particular emotion related, though the child may verbalize a rudimentary notion that death is connected with sorrow or sadness.

3

5 Years:
- Concept of death becomes more detailed, accurate and factual.
- May still think death is reversible.
- May develop bodily actions that are associated with death—child avoids dead things or may enjoy killing bugs, for example.

6 Years:
- New awareness of death. Children begin to develop an emotional response to the idea of death.
- Fear that their mother will leave them.
- Idea that death is the result of aggression or killing.
- Some preoccupation with graves, funerals and burial.
- Do not believe that they will or can die.

7 Years:
- Perception of death is similar to six-year-olds, but it is more detailed and realistic and they have a better understanding of the situation.
- Children have an interest in the causes of death, old age, violence and disease.
- The child expresses an interest in visiting cemeteries.
- There may be complaints such as "I wish I was dead!"
- The child gets the notion that he or she may die but will usually deny this when confronted.

8 Years:
- Progresses from an interest in graves and funerals to interest in what happens after death.
- Feels that he or she has a better understanding of the concept of death.
- Still retains some "magical" thinking regarding death.

9 Years:
- References now made to logical or biological reasons for death. For example, "Not living is when you have no pulse and no temperature and can't breathe."
- Now looks straight at death, not just at the peripherals such as coffins and graves.
- Accepts quite realistically the fact that when they become old, they will die. (Adapted from Gesell 1941; Wolfelt 1983).

It seems clear that some common elements of grieving are usually found in children of any given age, although each child grieves in his or her own unique way. In general, children, age 5 and younger, think that death is not final. To them, separation and death are the same things; in their view, the departed person is in heaven, or maybe somewhere else on earth. The uncertainty regarding where a dead person "goes" is shown clearly in the following child's behavior. When David was 4, his father died. After his death, David began to bury food in the sandbox. When his mother asked him why he was burying food, David replied that it was for his father to eat.

Children, ages 6 to 9, understand that death is final but only to a point. They personify dead people as bogeymen, skeletons, or other fearsome creatures, and stories of devils or ghosts may frighten children for years. They may have vague ideas about the soul living on after death. For example, when Frank was 8, his father died and he became convinced that his father's soul had moved into a rabbit that lived in their yard. Frank became obsessed with taking care of the rabbit and could not sleep on cold nights for fear that the rabbit would freeze.

Karen, who is 7, illustrates how the concept of the soul can be confusing to a child. She was convinced that her grandmother had moved into her closet after she died. When Karen's mother asked her where Grandma lived in her closet, Karen explained that Grandma now lived on in the bottom of her best pair of shoes. Karen had apparently confused the words "soul" and "sole."

Children ages 10 and up have a fairly good understanding of death. They begin to see cycles in nature and life and also consider the idea that they may die. However, children older than 10 often question the social customs and rituals surrounding death. For example, when Mary's mother died, 11-year-old Mary thought it was stupid to buy a new dress for her mother's burial because "it [would] just rot."

Given that children have a different approach to grieving than adults, it would clearly behoove adults to develop meaningful ways of talking to children about death. In other words, adults need to know how to comprehend children's perception of death. The following are several methods for accomplishing this task. They include the Sentence Completion Test; the Thematic Photographic Book; Nurturing, Intruding, Structuring, and Challenging in Play Therapy; the Anecdotal Record; and the Grief Process Group for Adolescents.

The Sentence Completion Test (Ryan and Giblin 1988)

1. The most frustrating part of this particular death to me is . . .

2. One way I have changed since the death is . . .
3. I don't understand . . .
4. I miss the most . . .
5. I take responsibility for . . .
6. I would like my (remaining parent/s) to . . .
7. I like the way I have . . .
8. One thing that has changed for the better is . . .
9. If I could change one thing about myself now, it would be . . .
10. My friends feel . . . about our family situation.
11. One thing that I'm not doing now that I would like to do is . . .
12. One thing that I really appreciated about the person who died is . . .
13. My pet, since the death, misses . . .
14. My picture of the person I miss is . . .

The Thematic Photographic Book (Ryan and Giblin 1988)

Based on the work of Viorst (1987) and Pollack (1977), the Thematic Photographic Book should consist of recollections compiled from any previous losses that the child may have experienced before this present death. This book can include pictures of loss in nature, in relationships, of loneliness and anxiety in other life experiences and, ultimately, how this death-loss triggers the memory of previous losses.

PROCEDURES

Pictures are shown and the child is asked to tell a story about them. The therapist should record any basic themes and patterns he notices from the child's narrative. The pictures shown can be pictures of nature—such as autumn leaves, animals, aging persons, rituals for funerals, mothers, fathers, siblings, sick persons, as well as specific personal situations in the child's life that the therapist may be previously aware of.

Nurturing, Intruding, Structuring, and Challenging

Theraplay (Jerenberg 1979), originally the method of Austin Des Lauriers, is particularly helpful in understanding the needs of children who are experiencing a deficiency from significant adults in the following four groups: nurturing, intruding, structuring and challenging. The following activities are found in these categories:

Nurturing: cuddling, catering, pampering, holding, teasing, enjoying warm moments, fun, surprise

Intruding: stimulated, excited, aroused, delighted, gazed at intensely, invigorating moments

Structuring: comprehending one's own confines and the boundaries of the surrounding world and knowing normal boundaries as distinct from diffuse and rigid boundaries

Challenging: stimulation, arousal, a spirit of competition

PROCEDURES

There are two ways that this method can be used. One way is to use the following six stages of Theraplay in interaction with the mother, child, and therapist and then to provide feedback by videotaping the sessions and replaying them with the mother and therapist present. The six stages are: introduction, exploration, tentative acceptance, negative reaction, growing and trusting, and termination with preparation, announcement, and parting of the "relationship" (Jerenberg 1979). Theraplay is meant to be more action-oriented than talk and insight-oriented; it is fun but it is clearly defined as to time, space, and parent-therapist roles. The other way is to use the above-mentioned four functions to create an anecdotal record as a means of determining the needs of the child.

The Anecdotal Record

In the Anecdotal Record, the therapist determines the child's personal situation and problems, then the outcome, and by using the four functions—nurturing, intruding, structuring, and challenging—chooses the intervention method believed to be most appropriate.

The Grief Process Group for Adolescents

Composition of Group

1. All adolescents suffering from the same loss (for example, the death of a student in the class).
2. Group limited to one type of loss (for example, divorce).
3. Each adolescent group member has his or her own loss.

Steps in the Process

1. Learn each member's name.
2. Discuss the losses (ask everyone).

      a. Name a specific loss experienced in your life.
      b. How did this loss happen?
      c. How did you find out about this loss?
      d. What do you miss?
      e. What don't you miss (for example, anger)?
      f. If you could do it over, would you change anything
         (for example, examining feelings of guilt)?
    3. Intervention—Activity
    4. Closure—Extinction

Group membership may be determined in various ways. Sometimes all of the children in the group are suffering from the same loss. For example, an 8th grade child was shot to death. A loss group was formed which consisted of children from his class who needed to talk about their deceased classmate. Other times the children in the group may have suffered the same type of loss, but their losses have occurred at different times and in diverse manners—a group of children whose parents have been divorced would comprise such a group. In this way, the children could share their experiences. A third way to compose a grief group is to put together children who have had a loss despite the type of loss they have experienced. For example, at one school a child had died and a few of his classmates were assembled for grief work. The counselor chose to add other children who had recently lost a parent: all the children in the group had experienced a loss and were able to relate to each other on the same topic.

    Once the membership of the group has been determined and the group has been assembled, the process is fairly straightforward. The leader puts forth questions such as the ones listed in the outline. Each child is asked to respond to every question, thus giving the more quiet children a chance to express themselves and giving all the children an opportunity to hear the experiences of the others.

    The questions should begin with the explanation of the loss. Most children are anxious to talk about the loss experience and rapport with the group and with the therapist will develop rapidly. Then, the group leader can move to the questions that the children may be more reticent to discuss: "What don't you miss about the person?" This question is asked to facilitate the potential expression of anger. Another difficult question is, "If you could do it over, would you change anything?" By asking this question, the targeted emotion is guilt.

    The next step in this group process is intervention or activity. Interventions are limited only by the scope of the creativity of the therapist and the group members. Writing letters to the deceased is a very effective way for the children to say "good-bye" to their loved one. The group can then decide what to do with the letters; frequently, they will put these letters where they feel physically closest to the deceased. For example, one group member chose to take their letter to the lake and burn it there because their friend loved to go to the beach. Other interventions might include drawing pictures which express feelings, having a memorial ceremony, doing a project in honor of the deceased or listening to the favorite music of the deceased.

The goals of these activities are focused on the idea that the feelings involved in grieving need to be shared and for teens the most comfortable place to share those feelings is with their peers.

After the intervention has been completed, the leader should summarize what has happened within the group. As in all grief counseling, the group should not part until all the group members have been able to experience an emotional release or catharsis. In other words, emotions should not be left raw. A feeling of closure should exist before the group parts. Unfortunately, exactly when this closure will occur cannot always be determined, so these groups do not always fit into the schedules of schools where everything occurs within set time frames. For example, at one school where we led a group, the principal did not understand that after a schedule had been set, the possibility of change was probable and that time frames must remain somewhat flexible.

CONCLUSION

This chapter has shown the developmental characteristics applied to children's perceptions of death; various ways of reaching preschool children in their perceptions through play therapy; anecdotal records including nurturing, intruding, structuring, and challenging functions, the Sentence Completion Test (Ryan and Giblin 1988), and the Thematic Photograph Book; and for adolescents a model one-session Grief Counseling Group. It is hoped that the value of reaching the child's perception of death will bring about other creative strategies in assisting children deal with loss.

REFERENCES

Bowlby, J. *Attachment and Loss.* Vol. 1. New York: Basic Books, 1969.
Freud, S. *"Mourning and Melancholia."* In J. Strachey, ed., *The Standard Edition of the Complete Psychological Works of Sigmund Freud. Vol. 21.* London: Hogarth Press, 1957.

Gesell, A. *Developmental Schedules.* New York: The Psychological Corp., 1941.

Jerenberg, A. *Theraplay.* San Francisco: Jossey-Bass, 1979.

Pollack, G. The mourning process and creative organizational change. *J. Am. Psychoanal. Assoc.* 25:3–34, 1977.

Viorst, J. *Necessary Losses.* New York: Fawcett/Gold Medal, 1987.

Wolfelt, A. *Helping Children Cope with Grief.* Muncie, IN: Accelerated Press, 1983.

2

The "Adult" Concept of Death: Irreversibility

Mark W. Speece, PhD and Sandor B. Brent, PhD

Studies of the development of children's understanding of death typically compare the children's understanding against a presumed mature adult concept. This chapter examines the validity of one component of that adult concept—*irreversibility*—by comparing actual adult data to the presumed adult standard and to actual child data. One hundred and sixty five undergraduates took a self-administered questionnaire containing five questions concerning the irreversibility of death—whether death can be changed once it has occurred. Subjects answered each question by circling one of four responses: YES, NO, DON'T KNOW, or NOT SURE, and provided explanations for their answers. Interestingly, the adults as a group conformed less well in their answers to the presumed adult standard than did the children. However, the adults' explanations indicated that their lower conformation to the presumed adult concept was caused by a by-product of their more sophisticated understanding of the complexity of their present-day efforts to conceptualize exactly what boundary marks the transition from life to death. As well, implications for further study on the development of the concept of death are discussed in this chapter.

Over 50 studies have examined the development of children's understanding of death (Speece 1986; Speece and Brent 1984). These studies typically compare the children's understanding against a presumed mature concept of death. The underlying assumption of this comparison is that this mature adult concept is the end-state toward which the process of conceptual development is directed. However, the adult concept itself has never been empirically validated.

11

The three most widely studied components of children's concepts of death are universality, irreversibility, and nonfunctionality (Speece and Brent 1984). That study (as well as the study in this
chapter) focused on irreversibility. Irreversibility refers to the idea
that a living thing, once dead, can never become alive again—i.e.,
that death is an *unconditionally* irreversible process. An empirical
investigation of how adults actually understand the irreversibility
of death is of interest because irreversibility has generally been
assumed to be one of the principal components of a mature concept
of death.

Irreversibility was, and still is, of interest to us because 41
percent of the 3rd grade students in Speece's earlier study indicated that a dead person under certain conditions might be
brought back to life, while only 12 percent of the 2nd grade students endorsed this possibility. The fact that the older children
were also more likely than the younger children to give physiological justifications for their answers suggested the possibility that
this difference in the expected developmental trend (i.e., from life
to death), might be caused in the older children by a more sophisticated understanding of some of the complexities involved in
modern adult conceptualizations of the relationship between life
and death.

The study in this chapter was designed to examine the extent
to which adults, in fact, agree that death is *unconditionally* irreversible.

METHODS

A self-administered questionnaire was adapted from an interview
schedule used by Speece (1987) in a study of children's understanding of death. The questionnaire used in the present study, like that
in Speece's study, was designed to investigate all three principal
components of the concept of death: universality, irreversibility,
and nonfunctionality. However, the present report is only concerned with the five questions which made up the irreversibility
subtest of the questionnaire.

Questions

The first item in the questionnaire was the direct, general question,
"Can a dead person become alive again?" This was followed by
four specific questions: whether water, food, medicine, or magic,
respectively, could make a dead person alive again (see Table 1).
These four items are of interest because some children in previous

studies indicated that one or more of these methods might sometimes be effective in bringing a dead person back to life again.

Responses

Subjects were instructed to respond to each question in two ways: first by circling one of four choices (YES, NO, NOT SURE, or DON'T KNOW), then by providing an explanation for their circled response. We refer to these as the subject's *responses* and *explanations*, respectively.

SUBJECTS

One hundred and sixty five undergraduates from two universities—one a college of engineering, the other a college of liberal arts—completed this questionnaire. Subjects ranged in age from 18 to 50 years (M = 25.4). Fifty-eight percent were female, 42 percent male, 40 percent described themselves as Catholic, 34 percent as Protestant, and 12 percent as either agnostic, atheist, or "no religion."

Subjects were solicited from seven classes, representing five undergraduate psychology courses: The Psychology of Death, Dying, and Lethal Behaviors; The Psychology of Myth, Magic, and Religion; Developmental Psychology; Psychology of Personality; and Introductory Psychology. Two of the seven classes consisted primarily of engineering students and five primarily of liberal arts students. This relatively well-educated and intellectually sophisticated population was particularly appropriate for this study because it seemed likely that many would have already achieved a mature adult concept of death.

RESULTS

The results of this study are presented in three sections: a quantitative analysis of the subjects' basic responses; a qualitative analysis of their explanations for those responses; and a quantitative analysis of the relationship between their responses and their explanations.

Scoring

Each question was deliberately worded so that a NO response would indicate that the subject conceived of death in a manner consistent with the presumed mature adult response (see Table 1).

Thus, those subjects who conceived of death as *unconditionally* irreversible were expected to respond NO to all five questions, while those who conceived of death as *conditionally* reversible might respond YES, NOT SURE, or DON'T KNOW to one or more of these questions.

Recoding

Some subjects' circled responses were recoded on the basis of their written explanation. For the first question, "Can a dead person become alive again?" approximately 11 percent of cases (18 of 165) were recoded. In 13 of these cases, although the subject had circled YES, NOT SURE, or DON'T KNOW, it was clear from their explanations that they did not believe that the death of the physical body was reversible, but had answered in terms of spiritual continuation rather than physical reversibility. For example, one subject who circled YES for this question answered, "Spiritually he can, physically he cannot once dead." In these cases the subject's response was recoded as NO.

On the other hand, in three cases the reason given for the NO response clearly indicated that physical death was (or could be) reversible under certain circumstances (e.g., through medical intervention or through a miracle). In these cases, a NO response was rescored as a YES.

Table 1.
Percentage of Adults and Children Responding NO to Each Question of the Irreversibility Subtest and to All Five Questions

Questions	Adults (N = 165)	Children* (N=91)
1. Can a dead person become alive again?	55	93†
2. If I gave a dead person a drink of water, could he become alive again?	92	96
3. If I gave a dead person some food to eat, could he become alive again?	92	97
4. If I gave some medicine to a dead person, could he become alive again?	66	86†
5. If I said some magic words to a dead person, could he become alive again?	88	87
Percentage answering NO to all five questions	44	69†

*Adapted from data collected by Speece (1987).
†$p(X^2) < .001$; for all others $p > .05$.

Table 1 shows the percentage of adults who answered NO to each question—i.e., whose answers conformed to the presumed mature adult concept. Comparable data are shown for the kindergarten through 2nd grade children studied by Speece (1987).

While 55 to 92 percent of the adults answered NO to each question, only 44 percent answered NO to all five questions. Thus, a majority of these adults did not conceive of death as unconditionally irreversible in all of these aspects of irreversibility. Most had at least some doubts about whether or not one or more of these conditions might lead to a reversal of death.

Comparison of the adult data with the child data shows that for two of the questions, "Can a dead person become alive again?" and, "If I gave some medicine to a dead person, could he become alive again?" a significantly smaller percentage of adults than children conformed to the presumed mature adult standard. However, the reason for the adults' apparently less mature responses becomes clear from their explanations.

Explanations

For the sake of brevity we shall examine only those explanations which these adults gave for their responses to the general question "Can a dead person become alive again?" However, these data illustrate both the types of explanation the adults offered for all five irreversibility questions and the methods we used to analyze them.

One hundred and four subjects (63 percent) provided an explanation for their response to this question. A content analysis of these explanations resulted in the categories system outlined in Table 2. Because some explanations were quite complex, different parts of the same explanation might fit different categories.

There are two major groupings of explanations: the naturalistic and the non-naturalistic, and each contains several subcategories. In addition, several miscellaneous types of explanations are grouped in the "other" category.

NATURALISTIC EXPLANATIONS

Naturalistic (N) explanations are those that refer to the death of the physical body in the context of natural (scientific) laws. This category has six subcategories: medical, temporal, definitional, knowledge-based, explicit physical, and miscellaneous naturalistic.

Table 2.
Outline of Category System for Explanations
of Irreversibility Responses

I.   Naturalistic Explanations (N)*
    A. Medical (M)
    B. Temporal (T)
    C. Definitional (D)
    D. Knowledge-based (K)
    E. Explicit Physical (EP)
    F. Miscellaneous Naturalistic (MN)
II. Non-naturalistic Explanations (NN)
    A. Explicit Spiritual Continuation (ESC)
    B. Implicit Spiritual Continuation (ISC)
    C. Reincarnation (R)
    D. Eschatological Resurrection (ER)
    E. Supernatural Intervention (SI)
III. Other Explanations (O)
    A. Spontaneous Reversal (SR)
    B. Psychological Causality (PC)
    C. Miscellaneous Other (MO)

---

*Abbreviations are used in Tables 3 through 6.

Medical (M) explanations state that reversibility sometimes occurs (or might possibly occur) in a medical setting (e.g., a hospital) or through the use of medical techniques (e.g., CPR, resuscitation). The following response is an example of this mode of thinking:

> There have been cases where someone has been 'dead' for a couple of minutes and through medical techniques has been brought back to life: CPR, other medical equipment (life support machines).

Temporal (T) explanations state or imply that reversibility is (or may be) possible in some cases if the person has only been dead for a short time.

> I think there are some cases where a 'legally' dead person (a person whose bodily functions have ceased to function) can be brought back (e.g., by CPR). Beyond that I say no. I am therefore treating death as a person whose bodily functions and alpha waves have stopped functioning for more than 1 hour.

> Proper medical help that is fast enough.

> If the person's heart stops for a few seconds and they are resuscitated.

Definitional (D) explanations state or imply that death appears to be reversible under certain circumstances due to the way "death" or "dead" is defined, either personally, medically, or legally. The person may state the definitional issue explicitly or may indicate it implicitly, by placing quotation marks around the words "dead" or "death" or by using verbal qualifications such as "clinically" dead, "medically" dead, or "legally" dead. We inferred from these devices that the subject intended to imply a *special* usage of the words dead and death. For explanations in this category the definitional issue concerns the criteria used to determine whether the death of the physical body has actually occurred, rather than whether there is some type of spiritual continuation after the body dies.

> Of course there are instances when a said 'dead' person was brought back or simply came back to life (most often in an operating room) and have reported what they have seen. Their visions are what they believe to be true. No one else knows. My belief is that they were never dead.

> In hospitals it's happened, I believe, although the definition of 'dead' is not clear to me.

> My definition of a dead person is when the heart stops and the brain stops working. However, many times people have been brought back to life by the use of CPR or other resuscitation devices.

> There are a number of cases of people being pronounced 'clinically dead' only to recover and lead normal lives.

Knowledge-based (K) explanations state or imply that reversibility is impossible given our current state of medical knowledge or technology, but will (or may) be possible in the future, as a result of further advances in knowledge or technology.

> Medical technology is unable to find how to yet.

> Not at the present, but I believe this may be possible sometime in the future.

Explicit physical (EP) explanations explicitly state that death of the physical body is irreversible. We can infer from this the implication that death in some other sense may be reversible.

> Not in the biological sense, but perhaps in an afterlife, such as heaven.

> A dead body cannot become alive again.

Miscellaneous naturalistic (MN) explanations are those that did not fit into any of the aforementioned categories. There were, however, too few of these to form any additional categories at this time.

> Chemical reactions simply cannot reoccur after molecular destruction occurs. The chemical reaction process of life ends and is irreversible to higher forms.

NON-NATURALISTIC EXPLANATIONS

Non-naturalistic (NN) explanations are those that refer to (or imply) the possible existence of some supernatural process, force or being. This category has five subcategories: explicit spiritual continuation, implicit spiritual continuation, reincarnation, eschatological resurrection, and supernatural intervention.

Explicit spiritual continuation (ESC) explanations are those that both explicitly distinguish spiritual survival from physical death and explicitly state that spiritual continuation is (or may be) possible.

> Not in the biological sense but perhaps in an afterlife, such as heaven.
>
> Not physically, but maybe spiritually in another existence.
>
> Alive in a more abstract sense.
>
> Spiritually he never really dies. But when someone dies (heart stops, breathing stops), medical personnel, through medication, can make the heart start beating and breathing to resume.

Implicit spiritual continuation (ISC) explanations state specifically that "physical" or "biological" death is irreversible, but make no statement about any other forms of survival or reversibility after death. However, the explicit statement that the death of the "physical body" is irreversible is taken to imply that perhaps some other kind of death, or death in some other, non-physical sense (presumably in some "spiritual" sense) is (or may be) reversible. Explanations in this group were highly correlated, but not identical, with the explicit physical explanations described above.

> The physical body can no longer be brought to a functioning level.
>
> Once a physical body is dead, it's dead forever.
>
> Not physically, if ever.

Reincarnation (R) explanations refer to a type of spiritual continuation in which the soul/spirit enters a new (different) body.

> I believe so because I believe in reincarnation. The essence of life is not lost, but is renewed.

Eschatological resurrection (ER) explanations refer to a definite time in the future (the Last Day, the Last Judgment, the Second Coming of Christ) when all the dead will be resurrected at once.

> There could be some possibilities such as voodoo, black magic and the end of the world when the Bible says that God will rise [sic] the dead.

> If the world is recreated, those who are dead may come back alive in another form. The biblical method of God reshaping or reforming the world.

Supernatural intervention (SI) explanations state that an individual death is (or may be) reversible through some sort of supernatural intervention. The fact that reversibility involves the same physical body distinguishes this from reincarnation; the fact that it effects only a limited number of the dead, rather than all of the dead, distinguishes it from eschatological resurrection.

> With the exception of being dead for a couple of minutes and brought back to life in a hospital and a miracle, nothing.

> When an entity such as God interferes with death. When this being repairs what caused death.

> I have read where people have died for a short amount of time and come back to life. A person's will to live; the power of prayer.

OTHER EXPLANATIONS

Three categories of other (O) explanations did not fit into either the naturalistic or the non-naturalistic group: spontaneous reversal, psychological causality, and miscellaneous.

Spontaneous reversal (SR) explanations are those in which death is (or may be) reversible without the intervention of any specific agent or activity.

> There are no methods, it's just something that can happen. If a person's heart has stopped beating for more than a few seconds then the person is dead and if the heart starts beating again (with aid or not) the person is alive again.

Psychological causality (PC) explanations are those in which death is (or may be) reversible if the dead person wills it to be, thus extending the possibility of psychological causality beyond the moment of death.

> Medical methods or the person's will not to die can contribute to their returning back to life.
>
> Strong will; strong body before he died.

Miscellaneous other (MO) explanations: all remaining explanations, including ambiguous explanations, were placed in this category.

> From ashes we come; to ashes we shall return.

Relationship Between Responses and Explanations

In this section we explore some quantitative relationships between subjects' responses to the question "Can a dead person become alive again?" and explanations for these responses.

PROBABILITY OF GIVING AN EXPLANATION

While every subject circled a response to this question, not all gave an explanation for their response. As well, the distribution of explanations across response groups was not uniform. Table 3 shows both the distribution of subjects across the four response groups and the percentage of subjects within each group who gave an explanation for their response. Three aspects of these data are of particular interest.

First, only 11 of these 165 adult subjects (6 percent) expressed no opinion on the matter (i.e., DON'T KNOW). The remaining 154 (94 percent) all expressed some opinion. Second, those subjects

Table 3.
Percentage of Subjects in Each Response Group
Giving Explanations for Their Responses

Response Group	Number of Subjects in Response Group	Percentage Giving Explanations
YES	42	90
NOT SURE	30	90
NO	82	41
DON'T KNOW	11	45
Total	165	63

who circled YES or NOT SURE—in other words, those who indicated that a dead person could (or might be able to) become alive again—were twice as likely to give a written explanation as those who answered NO or DON'T KNOW. This suggests that those who answered NO believed their reasoning was self-evident and, therefore, felt no need to give an explanation, while those answering YES or NOT SURE recognized that the reasons for their answer might not be evident to the researcher, and, therefore, felt obliged to give some explanation. This, in turn, suggests that implied in the tendency to give an explanation for a response is the subject's understanding that that response did not in fact conform to the presumed adult standard and therefore needed some justification or elaboration.

NATURALISTIC, NON-NATURALISTIC, AND OTHER EXPLANATIONS

Table 4 shows the percentage of subjects in each response group who gave each major type of explanation: naturalistic (N), non-naturalistic (NN), and other (O). Because so few subjects responded DON'T KNOW, the data for this group is considered highly unreliable. Although they are included in this and the following tables for the sake of completeness, we will omit this group from our discussion. Two observations are of interest here.

First, the number of subjects in the three most common response groups (NO, YES, and NOT SURE) who offered naturalistic, non-naturalistic and other types of explanations, respectively, were about the same: 76 to 84 percent of each group offered naturalistic explanations, 26 to 41 percent offered non-naturalistic explanations, and 13 to 24 percent offered other types of explanations.

Second, as the subjects' response goes from YES to NOT SURE to NO, there is a slight but steady decrease in their tendency to give

Table 4.
Percentage of Subjects in Each Response Group
Giving Each Major Type of Explanation

Response Group	Number of Subjects	Type of Explanation		
		N	NN	O
YES	38	84	26	13
NOT SURE	27	78	33	22
NO	34	76	41	24
DON'T KNOW	5	0	80	20
Total	5	76	36	19

naturalistic explanations for their responses and a steady increase in their tendency to give non-naturalistic and other types of explanations.

TYPES OF NATURALISTIC EXPLANATION

Table 5 shows the percentage of subjects in each response group who gave each type of naturalistic explanation: medical (M), temporal (T), definitional (D), knowledge-based (K), explicit physical (EP), and miscellaneous (MN).These data show clear differences between the three main response groups. Those subjects who answered YES to the question of whether or not a dead person could become alive again, primarily gave medical considerations as the basis for their responses and secondarily, temporal and definitional considerations.

Those who were NOT SURE were less concerned with medical and temporal considerations, but equally as concerned with definitional considerations. This suggests that perhaps what they were "not sure" of was the specific medical facts (the techniques and time intervals, for example) that might affect a death and cause the possibility of reversal in these situations.

Finally, those subjects who responded NO—i.e., they felt that a dead person could not become alive again—gave the fewest definitional and temporal considerations and, by far, the greatest number of explicit physical considerations. In particular, this latter group tended to respond with statements like, "not bodily" or "not physically," thereby implying that a dead person might become alive again in some other non-physical or non-bodily way—perhaps spiritually. As we noted above, so few subjects responded DON'T KNOW that the results for this group are probably unstable and therefore questionable. Nevertheless, it is striking that not one

Table 5.

Percentage of Subjects in Each Response Group Giving Each Type of Naturalistic Explanation

Response Group	Number of Subjects	Type of Naturalistic Explanation					
		M	T	D	K	EP	MN
YES	38	66	32	39	0	8	0
NOT SURE	27	44	11	41	7	7	0
NO	34	21	21	15	9	38	15
DON'T KNOW	5	0	0	0	0	0	0
Total	39	42	21	30	5	17	5

of the five subjects in this group gave even one naturalistic explanation.

These results show that most adults whose responses appear to conflict with the presumed mature adult standard (i.e., those who answered YES or NOT SURE) did, in fact, conceive of the death of the body as ultimately irreversible. The ambiguity, for most of this group, was posed by those people who felt that contemporary medical practice can possibly reverse the death of persons who have been judged to be dead for only a very brief time. The uncertainty confronting our subjects in these cases was frequently deciding just how long a person had to be dead before the process was truly irreversible.

TYPES OF NON-NATURALISTIC EXPLANATION

Table 6 shows the percentage of subjects in each response group who gave each type of non-naturalistic explanation: explicit spiritual continuation (ESC), implicit spiritual continuation (ISC), reincarnation (R), eschatological resurrection (ER), and supernatural intervention (SI). These data show both unexpected similarities and striking differences between the three principal response groups.

Surprisingly, about the same proportion of each of the response groups (12–15 percent) indicated some belief in the possibility of some sort of explicit spiritual continuation after the death of the body. This was surprising since the three principal response groups (YES, DON'T KNOW, and NO) differed so markedly with regard to most of the naturalistic explanation categories.

Equally surprising and interesting, is the fact that each response group appears to be associated with a different one of the remaining non-naturalistic explanations: Explanations which in-

Table 6.
Percentage of Subjects in Each Response Group Giving
Each Type of Non-naturalistic Explanation

Response Group	Number of Subjects	Type of Non-naturalistic Explanation				
		ESC	ISC	R	ER	SI
YES	37	13	0	3	11	3
NOT SURE	27	15	0	19	0	7
NO	33	12	27	0	0	3
DON'T KNOW	5	0	0	0	0	0
Total	102	13	9	9	6	5

dicated an implicit spiritual continuation (ISC) after death were most likely to be given by subjects who answered NO (i.e., a dead person could not become alive again), while explanations which referred to reincarnation (R) were most likely to be given by subjects who answered that they were NOT SURE whether a dead person could become alive again. Finally, explanations which referred to some sort of eschatological resurrection (ER) were most likely to be given by subjects who answered YES (i.e., a dead person could become alive again).

DISCUSSION

The question we originally asked was whether the putative mature adult concept of death as unconditionally irreversible is a valid representation of how adults actually conceptualize death. As mentioned in the opening of this chapter, this question is of special interest since studies of the development of children's understanding of death have typically compared children's understanding against this presumed mature adult concept (Speece and Brent 1984). In addition, Speece's (1987) study of children's concepts of death suggested that 3rd grade students' conceptualizations of certain aspects of irreversibility conformed less well to this adult standard than did those of 2nd grade students. The older children's explanations in this earlier study suggested that the decreased conformity of their simple YES/NO responses to our questions concerning the irreversibility of death were in part a result of their having developed a more complex understanding of the relationship between physiological processes and death than that possessed by the younger children.

Many of the adults in the present study, like many of the older children in the earlier study, were less clear than the younger children as to whether death is, in fact, reversible. These results support the general conclusion that for many adults the concept of irreversibility is a complex one, involving both naturalistic and non-naturalistic considerations. This complexity appears grounded, in part, in certain ambiguities which modern medical technology has introduced into adults' consideration of where to locate the boundary between "living" and "dead." In attempting to decide whether "a dead person could become alive again" these adults took into account such factors as the availability of medical technology, the length of time the person was in the death state, and the legal, clinical or ethical definitions of the distinction between "dead" and "alive."

RECENT DEVELOPMENTS IN ADULT
CONCEPTUALIZATIONS OF DEATH

The ambiguities concerning the reversibility of death expressed or alluded to by the adults in the present study appear to represent a relatively recent advance in how mature adults conceptualize death. Until about 20 years ago most adults seem to have conceptualized the boundary between alive and dead as well-defined and stable. The transition from the alive to the dead state was marked by the cessation of all respiratory and cardiac functions to the extent that those functions were detectable through the use of the medical technology available at that time which has primarily been the stethoscope. When there was no longer any detectable heartbeat or breath the person was considered officially dead. Finally, death was conceptualized as unconditionally irreversible. For convenience, we refer to this as the "premodern adult conceptualization of death." This premodern conceptualization was the prototype for the assumed mature adult concept of death used as the standard in most studies of the development of children's concepts of death.

Since the 1960s advances in medical knowledge and technology have radically altered these relatively simple and straightforward conditions. The use of sophisticated sensing devices have made it possible to detect the continuation of various bodily functions for some time after both heartbeat and respiration are no longer detectable by traditional means. At the same time, the development of CPR and other resuscitation techniques have made it possible to "bring back to life" persons who previously would have been judged to be irreversibly dead. Finally, the use of such devices as respirators and heart-and-lung machines has made it possible to artificially continue the cardiopulmonary functions of persons who under the premodern conceptualization would have been presumed irreversibly dead.

As a result, those conditions which previously marked the transition from alive to dead have become considerably more complex and the determination of exactly when a person passes from the alive to the dead state considerably more problematic. This ambiguity showed up in the present study in the responses of those subjects who indicated that whether or not death was reversible was a matter of "time" or of "definition."

Nolan (1987) has described this modern dilemma eloquently:

> Death's permanence bounds life's transience and consists of irreversible losses of bodily functions. At the borders of irreversibility,

however, lie the shadowy regions where functions may be lost and
regained, and where modern resuscitative skills interrupt the cycle
of functional losses that once led inevitably to death. . . .

Historically, loss of cardiac and respiratory function has defined, from the moment of its occurrence, an irreversible condition:
death. A person whose heart no longer beat and who no longer
breathed was dead.

The advent of modern resuscitative techniques changed this
reality, giving resuscitation a curious and symbolically problematic
kinship with death. The ability to succeed with resuscitation has
forced definitions of death to incorporate the additional element of
duration. "Death" no longer necessarily occurs at the instant the
heart and lungs cease to function. In fact, the potential for reversal of
loss of cardiopulmonary function makes it impossible to ever identify the precise moment of death.

The well-defined stable boundary line of the premodern conceptualization has been replaced by a region of ambiguity. This represents a new state, of indefinite duration, during which the person is
incapable of autonomous cardiovascular functioning, but may,
with the assistance of various life-support machines, continue to
maintain other vital functions. While this ambiguous state is still
separated from the unambiguously dead state by a well-defined
boundary, the boundary that separates it from the unambiguously
alive state is less well defined.

In addition, entry into this ambiguous state is marked by the
loss of autonomous cardiopulmonary functioning. But the processes involved in crossing this boundary are, in principle,
reversible—e.g., a person who has entered this ambiguous state
may become unambiguously alive again by cardiopulmonary
resuscitation. Thus, the boundary one crosses when entering the
ambiguous state is like that of the premodern adult conceptualization of death in that it is marked by the cessation of autonomous
cardiopulmonary functioning. However, it differs from that of the
premodern conceptualization in that it is only conditionally
(rather than unconditionally) irreversible: an individual may,
under appropriate conditions, pass back and forth across it.

Finally, although the modern conceptualization, like the premodern, includes a boundary beyond which even the most
advanced current medical knowledge cannot bring a dead body
back to life, the exact location of even that boundary may not be
permanently fixed. This is because future advances in medical
knowledge or technology may eventually push it out even further,
thus widening the region of indeterminacy still further. This ambiguity showed up in the present study in the responses of those

subjects which indicated that further advances in medical knowledge might someday enable us to bring back to life again many people who are today judged to be irreversibly dead.

IMPLICATIONS FOR CHILDREN'S CONCEPTUALIZATION OF DEATH

These changes in the adult conceptualization of the reversibility of death have important implications for the study of the development of children's concepts of death. Traditional studies of the development of the concept of death during childhood have assumed that one of the end-states of this development process would be the realization that death is unconditionally irreversible—an assertion that, it was assumed, most mature adults would endorse. This study examined the validity of the putative mature adult conceptualization. However, the results of the present study, taken in conjunction with those of Speece (1987), suggest that from about 9 or 10 years of age onward the development of the concept of death is directed toward a much more complex and sophisticated understanding of the relationship between life and death than that assumed in the traditional studies of this process. In particular, from about age 9 or 10 onward children seem to have a growing understanding of the fact that under certain conditions certain physiological states traditionally associated with unconditionally irreversible death may, in fact, be reversed by various medical procedures—an assertion which a significant number of the relatively well-educated and well-informed adult subjects in the present study freely entertained.

SUMMARY AND CONCLUSIONS

This study explored the validity of one component of the presumed mature adult concept of death: irreversibility. This question was of interest because most studies of the development of children's concepts of death have used this presumed adult concept as both the end-state toward which the children's development was directed and the standard against which the children's level of development was measured. These studies typically assumed (either implicitly or explicitly) that a mature adult concept would include the notion that death is *unconditionally* irreversible. However, our own earlier studies of children's concepts of death led us to question the validity of this assumption.

The results of the present study suggest that the mature adult concept of death as unconditionally irreversible is itself currently undergoing a developmental change. Recent advances in medical knowledge and technology have interposed between the states of being *unambiguously alive* and *unambiguously dead* and the new state, that of being *ambiguously alive*—i.e., alive only by virtue of the use of such heroic life-support measures as heart-and-lung machines and respirators. The ethical, moral, and legal status of the medical care provided to or withheld from persons in this ambiguous state are, of course, matters of great concern to many contemporary adults. These developments in the mature adult conceptualization of death seem likely to influence the development of contemporary children's conceptualizations of death, as well. Hence, future investigators may be required to use a new, more complex and sophisticated standard against which to measure the development of children's conceptualizations of death.

REFERENCES

Carey, S. *Conceptual Change in Childhood*. Cambridge MA: MIT Press, 1985.

Kastenbaum, R. *Between Life and Death*. New York: Springer, 1979.

Moody, R. A. *Life after Life*. New York: Bantam, 1975.

Nolan, K. In death's shadow: The meanings of withholding resuscitation. *Hastings Center Rep.* 17(5):9–11, 1987.

Speece, M. W. "Children's Concepts of Death: A Review of Three Components." In G. H. Paterson, ed., *Children and Death: Proceedings of the 1985 King's College Conference*. London, Ontario: King's College Press.

Speece, M. W. The Development of Three Components of the Death Concept. (Doctoral dissertation, Wayne State University, 1987.) *Dissert. Abstr. Int.* 48:1170B, 1987.

Speece, M. W. and Brent, S. B. Children's understanding of death: a review of three components of a death concept. *Child Dev.* 55:1671–1686, 1984.

II

Care of the Dying Child

3

Dying Hmong Children: A Clash of Cultures

Dorothy J. Landis, MSW, ACSW

The crisis of a child's sudden critical illness or accident forces families to make decisions of enormous importance and to cope with great amounts of stress in an unfamiliar environment. When the child's family is from another culture, the challenges for helping the family through this crisis are multiplied. The purpose of this chapter is to examine the experiences of Hmong families in a pediatric intensive care unit in an American hospital. By looking at the factors that contribute to the stress these families experience, a framework is developed for understanding and intervening effectively with minority culture families of dying children. As well, implications for planning an intervention for all families with a suddenly-dying child are explored.

THE CRITICAL CARE EXPERIENCE

While some families have the benefit of knowing in advance that their child will have to be admitted to the hospital (and sometimes even an intensive care unit)—such as when surgery is needed and has been previously scheduled—others don't, and have to bear the fear of sudden hospitalization. The pediatric intensive care unit (PICU) experience will be examined in this chapter from the point of view of the family who enters a PICU with a child who has suddenly become ill or has just been injured to the degree that they require intensive medical care immediately.

Typically, such patients enter the PICU either from the emergency room or directly following transport from another hospital. The family has usually already been physically separated from the patient either in the emergency room or during transport. When patients enter the PICU there is often an initial period of time when the family is asked to wait in a waiting room while medical procedures are performed on the patient. Understandably, this is a period of great anxiety for family members of the sick child.

Once the family members are permitted to see their child (visitors are usually limited to two people at a time), they are confronted with a wide array of medical equipment and paraphernalia (for example, IVs, lead lines and monitors, catheters, tubes, a respirator and an intracranial pressure monitor). If the patient is on a respirator, he or she may have been medicated to produce paralysis—another disquieting thing with which the family will be confronted. To facilitate various procedures the child may have some distortion of his face, such as when the mouth is taped to accommodate a respirator. Normally active children are either often quite still, or else moving in an agitated, abnormal way. There can be an overwhelming number of unfamiliar visual stimuli, as well as the strange sounds of monitors, IV pumps and other machines that may look and sound frightening to the family.

Not only is the child's environment unfamiliar and stressful to the family, but if they are to remain near the child at all (that is, in the hospital, but not necessarily in the room), they must talk to one another in places that are unfamiliar and lacking in privacy (waiting rooms, cafeterias). Families can feel quite powerless in this situation, especially since the child's care has been almost entirely handed over to strangers.

As well, the necessity to make many, and sometimes immediate decisions adds greatly to family stress. Not only has the hospitalization been sudden and unplanned, but once the child is critically ill, decisions must be made quickly and at a time when the family's capacity for thinking and problem-solving is usually greatly diminished.

CULTURAL FACTORS FOR HMONG FAMILIES

Having a suddenly critically ill or injured child in an intensive care unit is extremely stressful in itself. Due to cultural factors, stress levels for Hmong families are even greater.

It is believed that the Hmong people originated in China and moved into the mountains of Laos over 150 years ago. There they established small villages high in the mountains. The Hmong were a rural, isolated people with little exposure to western science. During the years of war, between 1955 and 1975, there was considerable relocation and disruption of daily life (Koumarn 1979). While they aided the American military in the war, this affiliation in combat did not provide any significant exposure to western science.

After the pullout of U.S. forces from Southeast Asia, many Hmong made the dangerous journey to Thailand, where they stayed in refugee camps until they were able to emigrate to a country that would accept them, such as the United States. There are still many Hmong in camps in Thailand waiting for clearance to leave and enter another country. Thus, the immigration of Hmong into the United States (as well as other countries) continues and so Hmong are still arriving with life experiences that leave them ill-equipped to deal with western medical systems.

Perhaps the most striking contributor to the crisis of a Hmong family in a western hospital is the vastly different view of the disease process that the Hmong, not unlike other immigrants from Southeast Asia bring with them—a view often unrecognized by health care staff.

For the Hmong, explanations for illness may fall into four categories (Culhane-Pera 1988). The first is the natural explanation, in which the search is for an immediate, visible cause of the symptoms, such as bad food or water, weather, or accidents. The second theory of causation of illness is metaphysical. The hot and cold theory holds that

> in tune with nature, the human body operates with assumptions of a delicate balance between two basic opposite elements. . . . In medicine, the two poles become Hot and Cold, and health is the perfect equilibrium of hot and cold elements resulting from the harmonious functioning of the viscera (Tung 1980, p. 13).

The third explanation is a supernatural one and has to do with animistic beliefs. In traditional Hmong thinking, there are numerous *tlan*, or spirits, which can be classified by their functions (Barney 1979). Disease, in this belief system, is a manifestation of supernatural powers. Souls can come and go from the body. Illness can result from soul loss, the will of evil spirits or ancestral spirits or simply an ending of the mandate of life (Culhane-Pera 1988). It can be punishment by a spirit for an act which has violated a religious or ethical code or for an accident that has displeased a spirit. A fourth explanation is the enlistment of spirits by malevolent humans for evil purposes. Of all these explanations, the supernatural is the most favored by the Hmong, in particular that of soul loss (Koumarn 1979). The soul, or *pli*, is thought to be attempting to leave the body of the sick person. If that person becomes unconscious, the soul has departed and will leave for good unless it can be brought back.

Related to these beliefs are traditional treatments, including herbal medicine, maintenance of hot/cold balance through adjustment of diet, dermabrasive practices, massage, and spiritual means (Muecke 1983). Dermabrasive practices can be used to relieve such symptoms as headaches, colds, sore throats, breathing problems, diarrhea and fever. Cupping is one such technique. In this method a cup is heated and placed on the skin. The Hmong believe that as it cools, it contracts and draws the skin and excess energy (toxicity) into the cup. A circular ecchymosis is usually left on the skin. Another method is pinching, which can produce welts and bruises that may be seen at the base of the nose, between the eyes, and on the neck, chest, and back. A third method is rubbing, which involves the persistent rubbing of lubricated skin with a spoon or coin to bring toxic wind to the surface of the body. A fourth practice is burning, in which a lit cigarette or an ignited piece of cotton is touched to the skin, usually the abdomen, to compensate for the "heat" lost through diarrhea (Meucke 1983).

Spiritual treatment can include placation, use of herbs, or engaging the services of a shaman or *txiv neb*. A shaman, a priest who uses magic to cure the sick, can be male or female. Ceremonies may involve the burning of spirit money, sacrifice and the tying of strings to keep the soul from escaping the body. A shaman may conduct a ceremony in which he or she goes into a trance and travels to the spirit world to determine what is needed to cause the soul to return and restore health (Culhane-Pera 1988).

IMPLICATIONS FOR TREATMENT

These different beliefs have a number of practical implications for treating Hmong children in a western medical setting. Before bringing the child to a hospital for western care, families may use traditional medicine for a long time, thus making the child present with a more advanced state of illness than would otherwise be expected. Hmong families may also want to try traditional medicine instead of treatments recommended by physicians once the child is in the hospital, even when they are informed that their child is critically ill.

Permission for surgery for a critically ill child can be very difficult to obtain for a number of reasons. The Hmong traditional belief system holds that persons will live for eternity in the afterlife in the same state they are in at the time of death; thus, they prefer that the body is whole and intact at death. It is also believed that souls inhabit the various parts of the body and that the removal of any part of the body will result in a deprivation of some of the life force of that person. Also, they believe that a person (adult or child) who is disfigured or disabled has become this way either because spirits have inflicted it or at least they have not intervened to prevent it. Thus, this person does not have much "good luck," and can bring bad luck to others. A fourth issue is that if a family member grants permission for surgery and child dies, the family can be the object of revenge by the spirit of the deceased. The dead have power and if they have lost a body part through surgery, they may be even angrier. General anesthesia is yet another barrier to obtaining permission from the Hmong for surgery. Sleep, it is believed, can be a time in which the soul wanders from the body. Preternatural experiences can occur and therefore dangerous implications can exist for the individual. General anesthesia, in which a state of unnatural sleep is induced, is seen as especially risky (Culhane-Pera 1987).

Other beliefs make common western medical practices difficult for the Hmong to accept. The Hmong have high reverence for a person's head. It is considered to be the most important part of the body and the foundation of life. A person's head is traditionally seen as very personal, vulnerable, honorable and strictly untouchable except by close intimates. The Hmong believe that the invasion of any surface or orifice of the head may frighten and provide exits for the individual's life essence. Infants are considered at high risk for loss of life. This is particularly important, since IV lines may be placed close to the soft fontanel, from which it is believed that the soul may easily exit. Of great relevance is the belief held by the Hmong that western medicine simply may not work on an eastern person (Muecke 1983).

In addition to a different world view of health and illness, Hmong families usually bring with them language and cultural barriers that, especially in a crisis, can complicate their understanding of and ability to negotiate with the western health care system. Hmong family members may vary in their English fluency, from virtually no understanding of or ability to express themselves in English, to a good, functional understanding and use of English for everyday situations. Women who have been relatively isolated at home and men who have remained unemployed may be particularly limited in their English fluency. In some cases some family members will be dependent on others in the family for interpretation, and at other times all of the family members will need an interpreter. Because this service is provided by the hospital, the times when the interpreter is present is limited. This, of course, can increase the family's sense of frustration and powerlessness. Even for those Hmong whose English fluency is quite good, terminology used in a medical setting may be puzzling and is likely to be misunderstood. This problem is further complicated by the fact that Hmong people will often smile and nod as a cultural expression of politeness. This, however, may be misinterpreted by western health care staff as an indication that they understand.

In traditional Hmong culture, the family is more important than the individual and this is reflected in the decision-making process. Important decisions are usually made by a family group and in particular by the males. The male with the highest status is often the oldest male on the father's side of the family. A family's traditional method for decision-making can be disrupted when the members of the extended family are at different levels of acculturation. Younger family members and those who have been in the United States longer than others may be more acculturated and more accepting to western practices than older Hmong and newer immigrants. Sometimes the self-esteem of older family members is in jeopardy if they must rely on younger members for language interpretation, explanation and information.

When a child is critically ill, many Hmong family members—often the entire extended family—often gather at the hospital. Information and explanations are repeatedly sought as more and more relatives arrive. There is also often a desire to have many family members by the bedside and a wish to have someone in the family remain with the child at all times.

Another major problem is the mistrust that Hmong people may feel for western health care providers. Suspicion and mistrust are, in fact, a common phenomena among various groups of refugees (Culhane-Pera 1987). This mistrust may include beliefs that American doctors use Hmong children to experiment and try out procedures on so that health care personnel and trainees can learn and that when the money runs out from sources such as medical assistance, the doctors kill Hmong children. Mistrust of Americans by the Hmong can also probably be generated by the experience of having being virtually abandoned when the United States pulled out of Southeast Asia. When this happened, they were the victims of a great deal of violence.

Many people feel that of all of the Southeast Asia cultural groups, the Hmong took the greatest risks and suffered the largest number of casualties during the war while serving U.S. interests. In fact, virtually all of the tribal Hmong were involved in the war, acting as a major force in the northeast region of Laos (Indochinese Refugee Reports 1979).

By leaving their homeland in the mountains of Laos and finally settling in the United States, the current generation of Hmong adults have suffered tremendous amounts of loss. They and other Southeast Asian refugees from the Vietnam War are set apart from other Asian groups who have immigrated and resettled in the United States for a variety of reasons. First, they have come to the U.S. as a second choice. Their first choice would be to return to their homeland as it was prior to 1975. Second, they have come with very little, if any, preparation and few belongings. Third, there is no realistic chance for them ever to return to their homeland. And fourth, they are survivors. It has been estimated that for every refugee resettled, one died in flight (Muecke 1983). The Hmong who fled their homeland made long, dangerous journeys to reach the refugee camps in Thailand and many Hmong died or were killed by soldiers as they fled. Many of those who did reach the border of Laos and Thailand died crossing the Mekong River and those who did survive reached the camps with few possessions. The Hmong refugees who have resettled in America have experienced a staggering number of losses: family members, home and homeland, possessions and the myriad of common experiences they were used to in their native land, where they were once part of the main culture. Educated individuals who enjoyed high status in their homeland may be unemployed and isolated in American culture. As Lamb (1987) put it, "Everything but life is lost." It is probably safe to assume that most Hmong adults are suffering from a bereavement overload. Thus people already dealing with enormous amounts of loss and grief are faced with yet another potential loss when their child is brought to a PICU.

WESTERN HEALTH CARE STAFF PERSPECTIVES

For western health care staff, the same language and cultural barriers that the Hmong experience can be a problem. It can be quite frustrating to be unable to converse freely in the same language. History-taking, for example, can be difficult. Though interpreters can be very helpful, rapport is lost when staff cannot converse with parents in the same language.

Staff have difficulty in understanding a world view so vastly different from their own. Even when educated as to the way

Hmong people may perceive health and illness, some staff may be unable to fully appreciate why those of another culture cannot understand and accept "our" way of thinking. Also, because of their different ways of perceiving and interpreting the world, the stage is set for conflict between staff and Hmong families. What for staff are "routine" medical procedures, such as blood draws and IV insertions, can produce opposition from the family and the need for extensive negotiation.

Staff feelings of helplessness triggered by the critical illness or injury and the possibility of the child's death can be further exacerbated by the impaired ability to communicate with the family because of both language and cultural barriers. While it is neither professional, functional nor morally right, stereotyping of a minority population such as the Hmong can also exist among some staff members. This can decrease staff's ability to work effectively with a family, especially during a time of crisis. Each difficult situation can reinforce this stereotyping to the point that it becomes a self-fulfilling prophecy. A situation of continued misunderstanding can evolve.

A PICU staff is trained to make decisions and to act quickly under the pressure of time. While there are many situations in which families are encouraged to take the time they need to make certain decisions, the experience of health care staff is that the Hmong require more time to make decisions in more situations than most other families with whom they work. Western health care staff often find the Hmong extended family's decision-making process cumbersome to deal with. In a PICU, staff are used to dealing with family systems where eventhough extended family members may be present for explanations and recommendations, the parents of the child remain the primary decision-makers. As noted previously, in Hmong families, male elders are the most influential family members and the child's mother may have little influence over the male-dominated decision-making process. Also, more time generally must be spent imparting information and answering questions, requiring more numerous and lengthy family conferences. To make matters worse, resistance to the recommendations of the physicians is typically much higher by Hmong families.

The final blow for health care staff comes when, despite their intense efforts both to save the life of the child and to communicate effectively with the family, the child dies and the family feels that the death of the child was caused by staff. This can be a very frustrating situation and can discourage staff in further efforts to work with Hmong families.

SOCIAL WORK INTERVENTION

As a social worker, my role on the pediatric intensive care unit is to provide emotional support and crisis intervention to families of children hospitalized on the unit. Given the situation of Hmong families in this setting, the focus of intervention is threefold: to work effectively with individuals and families as they struggle with their child's illness and possibility of dying and facilitate their decision-making processes; to help staff understand the experience of the family and to deal with their own feelings of powerlessness and frustration in relation to the family and the child; and to serve as a broker in the system—bridging the two systems of family and staff. In order to communicate with the Hmong family, an assessment of English proficiency must be made. An interpreter is obtained if needed. On some occasions family members can be used as interpreters, though for meetings in which medical information is discussed, a trained interpreter should be used.

When I meet the family I introduce myself in Hmong and tell them, also in the Hmong language, that I speak a little Hmong. Even if the family members speak English fairly well, this effort to speak their language helps to start a positive relationship with them. The role of the social worker in this setting is then clearly defined for the family; I am there to help them. I will help them get the information they need, wait with them during difficult times and help them to get what they need in the hospital. As with any family with whom I work, I acknowledge their feelings and demonstrate an attempt to understand and respond to their needs. The family is given information to help them function in the PICU setting, such as what health care staff will allow regarding issues such as visitation and why such rules are necessary. The family is told which facilities are available to them, such as the waiting room, telephones, and a room for parents to sleep in.

An attempt is made to meet the various relatives present, to determine what their relationship is to the parents of the child, as well as their status and role in the family system. Family members are asked by what name they prefer to be addressed. Once the family's structure is determined, attempts are made to work effectively within that system. For example, information will be addressed to the senior or highest-status male present. At the same time, emotional support is directed toward the child's parents and other relatives through such things as Hmong phrases (*tu siab*, I'm sorry), limited physical contact when felt to be acceptable to the individual, and, finally the acknowledgment of their difficult situation certainly helps.

The second major focus of intervention is with health care staff. Since I often spend more time with the family than any staff members, I can be helpful to health care staff in facilitating their understanding of what family members may be experiencing. As with other families and situations on the unit, I am also available as a listener and facilitator for staff feelings. Having the opportunity to express their feelings, especially frustration, in this way can help staff to interact more effectively with the family.

The third major focus of intervention is to serve as a broker in the system, facilitating the interface of family and staff. This is carried out in a number of ways. One way is to travel frequently between the family and staff, obtaining information for the family. This is particularly crucial during times when family members are asked to stay in the waiting room, because their child is undergoing certain medical procedures.

In some ways I act as a "cultural interpreter," explaining family beliefs and needs to staff and vice versa. By talking to the family, I am sometimes made aware of the reasons for their resistance to certain procedures. If staff are able to understand why resistance is occurring, they can sometimes lessen their contribution to power struggles.

Sometimes I serve as a direct negotiator between staff and family at times of conflict, as, for example, when the family objects to a blood draw. One of my most important objectives at such time is to model for staff how to communicate and negotiate with the family.

In acting as a broker between systems, I find scheduling to be a critical task. I arrange for meeting times and places, making certain that all the principal parties understand and accept the arrangements and sometimes actually bring together the appropriate parties.

A FRAMEWORK FOR INTERVENTION WITH MINORITY CULTURE FAMILIES IN A CRITICAL CARE SETTING

Aside from the specifics of the role of the social worker/broker in the PICU setting, health care staff in general can be helped to learn skills that will greatly facilitate their working effectively with Hmong families as well as other minority culture families. What follows are a number of practical suggestions for interacting with Hmong and other minority culture families in a critical care setting:

1. Interact with the family system in a manner that is compatible with their status hierarchy and decision-making process. This means determining who is the person accorded the highest status within the system and addressing that person directly. For families for whom the males are clearly the decision-makers, as is usually the case for the Hmong, that group should be addressed directly.

2. Communicate with family members in a verbal and non-verbal manner that is warm and respectful. While this is valuable with all families, it is especially helpful with Hmong families. A quiet, unhurried but purposeful demeanor is part of normal professional decorum that is particularly reassuring to Southeast Asians because it symbolizes characteristics that are highly valued among them, such as wisdom, good judgment and dignity (Muecke 1983).

3. Routinely explain why medical procedures are needed. This can help to combat the belief that medical procedures are being done so that medical students can learn or that children are being used for experimentation. As a corollary, the number of procedures performed should be kept as minimal as possible.

4. Whenever practical and comfortable for staff, allow one or two family members to be present for procedures. It is helpful at such times to have someone (such as the social worker/broker) present to explain to the family what is being done.

5. In making recommendations for treatment or procedures, explain the reasons thoroughly. Explanations of diagrams, x-rays and test results are helpful.

6. Listen, attempt to understand and acknowledge what family members say. This can increase the chances of the family listening to what you have to say.

7. Communicate acceptance of family members and respect for their point of view. Comments such as, "You are wise parents to have these concerns" and "You ask good questions," can help to strengthen the relationship between staff and family.

8. Make an effort to respond to family members' questions and comments and give information in ways that do not cause them to "lose face" or self-respect.

9. Accommodate and meet the needs of the family whenever possible. The more you can allow the family to meet their

own needs, the more likely they will be to respond to the recommendations of western medical staff. For example, it may be possible to allow some traditional healing practices to take place in the hospital. In this way staff can demonstrate that traditional and scientific western healing practices can work together. This type of accommodation can be especially important when it is clear that the child is most likely going to die. By allowing the family to engage in traditional healing practices, staff may decrease the family's fears and anxiety, as well as the perception that the child could have lived had traditional medicine been used.

10. Make sure that staff and the family are in agreement regarding which issues are negotiable and which are not. In a critical care setting not all things are negotiable. Some things must be done rapidly in order to save the child's life. Some medical procedures are best done without family members present. These procedures should be chosen carefully and the non-negotiability of the issue as well as reasons for it should be communicated clearly to the family.

11. Use interpreters whenever the family's ability to understand is in question, whether this is because of apparent lack of English fluency, high stress levels, or unfamiliarity with western medical concepts and practices. When using an interpreter be certain that everyone present—family, staff and interpreter—has a clear understanding of the role of the interpreter, which is simply to translate what is being said between staff and family. It is not to "convince" the family to do what staff members want. If the interpreter falls into the role of a persuader, it can have a negative effect on the family's willingness to use the interpreter and to negotiate with staff in general.

12. When using an interpreter, speak to and look at family members rather than at the interpreter. This will help to keep the role of the interpreter in proper perspective. As well, staff can more effectively pick up behavioral cues from family members in this way (Muecke 1983). One further caution when using an interpreter; stop frequently to allow for translation. Do not assume that the interpreter can remember all parts of long explanations. Suggestions for reducing ambiguity when speaking through an interpreter or directly with someone with minimal English fluency follow:

    a. Use basic words, speak in simple sentences and use nouns rather than pronouns.

    b. Paraphrase words that are important and may be easily misunderstood (for example, "workup") so as to be precise about the specific meaning intended.

    c. Avoid the use of metaphors, colloquialisms and idiomatic expressions.

    d. Learn and use basic words and sentences in the family's language.

    e. Check to make sure you are understanding what the other person is saying (Werner and Campbell 1970).

13. Accommodate and be aware of cultural practices or inhibitions when interacting with family members, as well as in treatment of the child. For example, in general Hmong women do not shake hands. Putting an arm around the shoulders of a Hmong person is considered rude, as is pointing a finger at someone. A waving motion or snap of the fingers to call someone is a sign of contempt. Strings tied around the neck and limbs have great spiritual significance for the Hmong. They are there to encourage the child's soul to stay in the body and may guard against evil *tlan* that might try to claim the child's life (Armour et al. 1981). If at all possible, these strings should be left in place, even during surgery.

14. While keeping in mind cultural generalities, recognize that each family is unique. Do not assume that what is true for most families will be true of the family you are helping. Particularly as the Hmong acculturate, one can expect to see more variation in their customs and belief systems.

ETHICAL ISSUES

Because there are so many different beliefs and variant practices within each minority culture there are a number of ethical issues to be considered when one is dealing with critically ill children.

Our society places a relatively high value on children and legally mandates that families be reported to child protection agencies when abuse or neglect is suspected. With a minority population such as the Hmong, the issue of medical neglect is particularly relevant. How do we balance respect for and accommodation of cultural beliefs and practices with what western medicine believes to be the right of the child to "appropriate" medical care? If traditional Hmong medicine is used too long and the child, in fact, comes to the hospital too late and dies—is this a case of medical neglect? Intent is not the relevant factor in determining what is reported to child protection agencies; the only determinant is the real or potential effect on the child.

Another ethical dilemma is one that is merely an extension of one that faces us generally as medical technology advances. Increasingly, western medicine has the ability to "save" lives, though the life that is saved is sometimes seriously compromised. This loss of the "former" child requires grieving and adjustment for the family. This can be even more of a problem for the Hmong, for whom disfigurement or impairment has serious social consequences for the individual and the family, as noted previously in this chapter.

As we encounter situations where "life support" can be ended, the waters can be further muddied. The idea of stopping efforts to save the life of a child may be incomprehensible to a Hmong family. In a case of brain death, where the patient is declared dead but appears to be alive because he or she is hooked up to a respirator, for example, the potential for misunderstanding and further mistrust is enormous. Why are western doctors suggesting that the machine that is keeping the child alive be stopped? This can certainly increase the paranoia described earlier. Further, one can imagine the consequences—what thoughts might be engendered— by a request for organ donation from a Hmong child on "life support" equipment.

As with all medical ethical issues, there are no easy answers. It is important, however, that health care professionals continue to raise questions and to carefully examine both the individual situations and the broader issues raised.

REFERENCES

Armour, M., P. Knudson, and J. Meeks, eds. *The Indochinese: New Americans.* Provo, UT: Brigham Young University Press, 1981.

Barney, G. L. "The Hmong of Northern Laos." In *Glimpses of Hmong History and Culture.* Indochinese Refugee Education Guides, National Indochinese Clearinghouse, Center for Applied Linguistics, 1979.

Culhane-Pera, K. Hmong refugees: reactions to surgery. *Refugee Mental Health Letter* 1, 1, 1987.

————. Hmong Traditional Medicine and Shamanism. Lecture given to the American Refugee Committee, February 23, 1988.

Indochinese Cultural Traditions in *Indochinese Refugee Reports,* Washington: American Public Welfare Association.

Koumarn, Y. S. "The Hmong of Laos, 1896–1978." In *Glimpses of Hmong History and Culture.* Indochinese Refugee Education Guides, National Indochinese Clearinghouse, Center for Applied Linguistics, 1979.

Lamb, L. and J. Westermeyer. Dealing with loss and grief among refugees. *Refugee Mental Health Letter* 1, 2, 1987.

Muecke, M. A. Caring for Southeast Asian refugee patients in the U.S.A. *Am. J. Public Health* 73(4):436–437, 1983.

Tung, T. M. *Indochinese patients*. Falls Church, VA: Action for South East Asians, 1980.

Werner, O. and D. T. Campbell. "Working Through Interpreters and the Problem of Decentering." In R. Naroll and R. Cohen, eds. *A Handbook of Method in Cultural Anthropology*. New York: Columbia University Press, 1970.

4

Living with Cystic Fibrosis: A Family Affair

Myra Bluebond-Langner, PhD

If there is one word that I hear parents use repeatedly to describe the first year following their child's diagnosis of cystic fibrosis (CF), it is "overwhelmed." Parents speak of being overwhelmed by the diagnosis and by what they feel they need to learn to do in order to care for their child—who is at that moment and for months or years to come a dying child. They also have their healthy children to consider: when to get them tested for CF, as well as what to tell them about their sick brother or sister. This is not to mention the added everyday tasks that cannot be ignored: cooking, cleaning, looking after other children and, of course, earning a living.

How do parents manage? How do families deal with it all? In their words—"with difficulty." But they really have no choice and somehow they must manage. This is no mean feat when one considers what these plagued families must deal with.

Cystic fibrosis is a genetic disease marked by increasing, albeit slow, deterioration and a fatal outcome. At the time of this writing, there is no known cure for this disease, but with early diagnosis and treatment, patients can be expected to live until early adulthood; the median age of survival is 19 years. Patients require long, daily treatments of physical therapy and medication and must pay constant attention to diet. Daily family life is often interrupted by trips to the CF center and the hospital for increased treatments due to pulmonary exacerbations. Each day, hours and dollars are consumed fighting an opponent which slowly, but inexorably, gains ground. One would assume that the disease would strain the physical, emotional and financial resources of families to the limit. To the contrary, my study indicates that the majority of families of cystic fibrosis patients appear to remain, at least for certain periods of time, very much like other families. How do they keep CF from totally disrupting their lives and occupying their minds? How do they try to achieve some level of control, some modicum of normalcy in the face of this omnipresent master?

In this chapter, I examine the various strategies families adopt to contain the intrusion that CF makes into their lives and the implications those strategies have for well siblings. The strategies I will describe are adapted over the course of the illness, accommodating changes in the patient's condition, as well as the family's situation. Similarly, the impact of the strategies on individual family members changes over the course of the illness.

PROGRESS OF THE DISEASE

Period I—Living and Coping During the First Year Following Diagnosis

In the weeks and months following the initial diagnosis of cystic fibrosis, two strategies begin to develop: what I call *routinization of CF-related tasks* and the *compartmentalization of information*. The routinization of CF-related tasks involves the integration of the tasks of CF care into everyday life. For example, for the parents of newly diagnosed young CF patients, this means putting therapy sessions on a regular schedule and limiting them to those times. Therapy involves pounding the chest and lungs to help loosen and move the thick mucus that accumulates in the lungs and hosts various infections. It can take anywhere from 20 to 40 minutes and is sometimes preceded by the inhalation of various agents intended to loosen the mucus or medications used to treat RAD (formerly called asthma) found in many CF patients.

Care requirements become a daily chore like any other—part of day-to-day-living. One mother, recounting what she does in the course of the day, began:

> I do my beds and while he is getting his mist, I dust. Then I give him his PT [physical therapy].

Through repetition, regularization and routinization, parents report a growing sense of mastery and control. A sense which, as one parent put it, "was stripped away when our child was diagnosed." Interestingly, the routinization of CF-related tasks contributes to the patient's and the sibling's view of CF, not so much as "an illness or sickness," but rather as "something you have to do things for."

> I mean, most of the time I forget she has [CF] 'cause the things [I do for her] become quite routine. Therapy in the morning is just sort of normal. I don't look at her as having [an illness] at all. I just forget about it.

In part, through the routinization of CF-related tasks, the ultimate questions that CF raises tend to become secondary problems. As one parent explained to me half jokingly:

> The questions are there, like your teeth are there when you lose them. But every time you floss your teeth, you don't think about the fact that if you don't floss your teeth, you may lose them.

Many parents also feel that the daily routines of physical therapy are not only useful, but also in the words of one father:

> A way of saying there is this condition of CF and it's got to be respected and this is what we are going to do to respect it.

Just as parents try to manage the care, so too do they try to manage all the information they receive. At the time of diagnosis and all through that first year, parents are bombarded with information. Everyone is telling them what to do and how to do it—professionals, family members and even strangers. Even with all the new information parents must absorb, it is common for them to begin an intensive quest for information, reading all they are given and even asking for more. Interestingly, many view the information given at the time of the initial diagnosis as the most credible information they receive. There are lectures, presentations, groups, books to read on everything from how to do physical therapy while preparing high-caloric foods for your sick child to how to have fun with your spouse and healthy children while coping with a chronically and terminally ill child. It is a giant task and it's no wonder that families feel overwhelmed.

The second strategy that emerges in Period I—the *compartmentalization of information*—now becomes important. It involves the processing and sorting out of information about the sick child. This is useful as a means of centering on those issues that need immediate attention and delaying attention to problems that become important later—such as the very real fact that their sick child is going to die. In the first year following diagnosis, parents report struggling with determining which place treatment regimes, protocols, symptoms, acute crises, the possibility of a cure, and now terminal prognosis, will and should occupy in their minds. Decisions, whether conscious or unconscious, are made about which and where various kinds of information should be stored in their minds. They ought to keep information about the requirements for care and the potential for cure in the forefront of their thoughts. Many parents feel that if they focus on the fatal prognosis, they will not "be able to provide therapy and help [their] child to grow in other ways." When parents speak to me about how they sort out all this information, they talk about how necessary the compartmentalization of information and feelings is not only "for [their] own sanity" but also for "getting things done."

> You just can't dwell on it [the dying] and at the same time live and work.

Compartmentalization of information does not mean that parents stop thinking about the disease, the efficacy of treatment or the prognosis. At best, the less time one spends thinking about negative aspects of CF, the better. At this time and for years to come, the difficult issues that CF raises may emerge in dreams, in reactions to movies, in days before clinic visits, on special occasions (birthdays and holidays), as well as with each decline in the child's development. At these times, parents find themselves "thinking about it all over again."

Period II—The Years Following the First Annual Examination to the First Exacerbation

With the first year behind them, parents report "relative calm, things back to the way they were—almost." Many say they feel "more in control" or "in control again." There is good reason for them to feel this way; by the end of the first year, in most cases, the patient is doing relatively well. Also, by this point, parents have mastered the care routines; survived "ups and downs" and "found a way, at least for now, to deal with it all," including attending to and caring for their other well children. The healthy siblings have their rightful place of importance again.

In Period II there is a real desire on each family member's part to "keep things the way they are." Perhaps it is not surprising that in the years following the first annual examination, families begin to establish a sort of distance from the present problems, as well as the inevitable outcome of CF. A third strategy begins to emerge, what I call the *avoidance of reminders of CF*. This strategy involves engaging in behaviors that allow one to establish or maintain distance from CF and its consequences. For some parents, the distancing occurs "quite naturally; almost unnoticeably." The following is a list of different parents' explanations of how they started to react to their child's illness at this stage:

> I stopped reading so much about it. I didn't go to the groups anymore.

> I stopped being directly involved with fund-raising.

> I got less interested [in the disease itself] and more interested in just dealing with her usual, normal school problems. I just didn't want to focus on CF. I think it was probably because she was doing well and I started to realize that I couldn't go on being this involved forever.

For others, the distancing and avoidance are quite deliberate and noticeable. Some begin to miss clinic appointments:

> We have these clinic visits regularly scheduled and I'm never sure how good an idea it is. It just brings it [CF] up when she—we—don't need to be dealing with it. I'm happier with fewer visits, so it's not so much of a thing, she can forget about it [when it's not bothering her].

Some fail to tell physicians about changes in the child's conditions or to ask about troublesome symptoms.

At this time, among all the families, there is a marked shift in their waiting room behavior. The socialization with others, so prevalent in the first year following diagnosis, is replaced by an increasing degree of civil inattention. One no longer hears parents talking about their children's treatment or progress. For some parents, this is quite deliberate; they choose not to talk to other families—"I don't want to hear their stories." One is also struck by the lack of dialogue between parents and children. At most there is a simple exchange after the patient is weighed. Parents may look at books, but do not read them. The children's play in the waiting room is unfocused. Conversations seem to be limited to issues of waiting and waiting room behavior. They sit lined up, staring. CF is not discussed.

Discussions about CF at this time are rare at home, as well. Parents of children with mild disease, two years beyond diagnosis, told me how the interview was the first time they had talked about the prognosis since the first year after diagnosis. There is little talk about the disease beyond what happened at a visit or what treatments are needed. "We'll talk about a new medicine, but not the other things."

The parent's reluctance to talk about the disease in more global terms, at this time, is quite understandable. As a parent remarked to me,

> Why should we, right now when she is doing so well? What would be the point of it?

For well siblings, however, this lack of discussion can mean not only the end of the acquisition of further information about their sibling's disease, but also may end the quest for further information altogether. Well siblings are dependent on parents and patients for information. At the time of diagnosis, well siblings may be too young to be given any but the most basic facts about CF. These facts are limited to what medications the patient will need to take, why he needs enzymes and concrete matters like when and why enzymes are given, therapy and, perhaps, that the cough is not contagious. Information about the genetic component is often omitted from early discussion with well siblings. In many cases, this is simply because the siblings are too young to understand. If they are old enough to understand, it may seem to be too frightening a fact to tell a healthy child that her brother or sister is going to die. When the patient is doing relatively well, the parents tend not to give any more information.

Hearing no further discussion among parents and seeing no change in the patient's condition, some well siblings, especially young ones, ask no more. Older siblings sometimes interpret their parents' silence as a desire not to discuss CF and even though they want more information, they may be reluctant to ask. Reactions from healthy siblings follow:

> Maybe I should ask, learn more, but I don't.

> I don't think they want to talk about it.

With the child relatively healthy, families work very hard at keeping CF from dominating their lives. Talk could disturb that delicate balance. In the words of one father:

> When you talk about, you think about it, and I think that's when you start to center your life around it.

> I don't want to hide it 'cause I know it's there and I accept it but on the other hand, I don't want to build my life around it and I don't

want to build my kids' lives around it. I want them to lead as normal
a life as possible.

The desire for a normal life is palpable. The fourth strategy, the
redefinition of normal, is a necessary measure for coping. This consists of extending the realm of normal life to accommodate the
patient's condition and the family situation. When the patient is
relatively healthy and the difference in appearance and activity
level between a well child and a child with CF is not that different,
little need be said or done to accommodate the patient's condition.
When this is the case, well siblings and parents often disavow the
differences between the patient and healthy children by calling
attention to aspects of the patient's life that are similar to the
healthy children's. Parents and well siblings frequently mention
the patient's athletic abilities and activities.

There is almost a formula to what parents and well siblings say
when describing the patient:

[Name of patient] is just like anybody else [any other child]. [He/
She] plays [name of sport].

Participation in athletic events is a measure of just how much the
patient is just like everyone else. Minimizing the patient's actually
terminal condition helps to maintain the patient's morale and
makes life seem more normal. As one well sibling said,

She's just like everybody else except she takes some pills when she
eats [referring to enzymes that must be swallowed with each meal to
aid the digestion of fats and the absorption of nutrients].

In many homes, the patient's enzymes, vitamins and some anti-
biotics are kept in the center of the kitchen table along with other
family members' vitamins.

Joking is also used to make life seem more normal. For example, CF patients burn off a large number of calories just breathing.
Also, food is not always properly absorbed and hence patients have
a greater food intake than the rest of us. Rather than intimate the
disease as a cause of a patient's voracious appetite, siblings often
joke, "He eats all the time 'cause he's a pig."

No one appears more invested in defining the family situation
as normal than the well siblings. Well siblings make a real effort to
minimize the patient's condition, to make sure that parents, peers
and strangers see the patient as normal—"like everyone else." This
is not surprising. First, being normal—which translates in Ameri-

can society as being like everyone else—is valued. No one knows this and works harder at it than children and should a child forget, his peers will be quick to remind him. As long as the patient is considered normal, well siblings feel justified in making demands for attention, privileges and special foods (like the ones the patient is getting).

As we will see, in the later stages of the illness when it becomes obvious that the patient is not like other children but instead seriously ill, well siblings feel less justified in making their demands directly known. As noted previously, this is not the case in the years following diagnosis when patients seem relatively healthy and look and act very much like other children. In early stages of the disease, well siblings clearly voice their demands for attention and special privileges. For example, one day in the clinic waiting room, two healthy brothers of a CF patient with very mild disease asked their mother if she would take them to get something to eat or let them go to the cafeteria on their own. The clinic was quite backed up and there was time before their sister would be examined. The mother said, "No. We'll wait until Zoe's been examined." The brothers replied, almost in unison, "If Zoe wanted something to eat, you'd go get it for her right away."

It is important to bear in mind that living a relatively normal life is possible and even expected when the child is doing well. Physicians encourage families to treat the patient normally and to get on with their lives.

When the sick child is relatively healthy and life has returned somewhat back to the way it was before the child was diagnosed, a fifth strategy, *reconceptualization of the future*, begins to emerge. Reconceptualization of the future involves the recognition that there really is only a limited future for the child with CF. At the time of diagnosis it seemed to be a situation without end.

In our society, when we look at children, we think of their future—a future almost without bounds, without limits, without end. Children and future could almost be considered synonymous terms. We see children as people who will grow and have a future. When children are diagnosed with a chronic, terminal illness, the future with all its opportunities is immediately dashed. For parents, finding out that their child has CF is like receiving a death sentence. As time and the illness progress, the absence of a future is commonly replaced by what the future really holds. It is not the one commonly associated with children in our society, rather one that is temporarily and qualitatively limited. The future may progress at least as far as high school graduation and maybe even college, a job, and marriage.

The first exacerbation of the disease marks the end of Period II. When the first exacerbation occurs, CF intrudes dramatically into the family's life, into their activities, thoughts and feelings. Established routines and "normalcy" are broken as more therapy is required and trips to the hospital become more frequent. Information about the course of the disease—lung deterioration and prognosis—carefully tucked in the parents' minds (Period I) now moves to the surface. The reality of the disease and its consequences abound as trips to the hospital to visit the patient increase. Visiting your child in the hospital is certainly not a normal, everyday event in an ordinary life. Now the future really seems limited. When the first exacerbation occurs, the sense of mastery and control that the family developed since diagnosis is severely undermined.

Period III—From Recovery from the First Exacerbation to Increased Hospitalization

Upon recovery from the first exacerbation, families again try to gain control by attempting to contain the intrusion CF has made into their lives, their activities, thoughts and feelings. The third period is marked by intensification of the aforementioned strategies, as well as making the changes necessary to accommodate the patient's condition. Therapy, which has in some cases slacked off, begins again with new zeal. New routines are established to accommodate the increase in the amount of therapies that come in this third period of more advanced illness.

New information acquired at the time of the first exacerbation is processed and sorted. Parents formulate a view of the disease that, as so many mothers say, "they can live with." While the chronic character of CF moves to the front of parents' minds, it is balanced by a sense that CF is "something we are going to [have to] live with." In the words of one father:

> It's funny, recovering from that pneumonia convinced me that the first time she got sick wasn't going to be it.

Many families continue their efforts to maintain distance from CF. Avoidance of reminders of CF continues. As in the second period, they do not talk about the disease in the waiting room or at home, despite changes in the child's treatment. They do not seek new information about CF. And in time, some start to miss appointments again.

In the third period there is a real desire to "hold on to what you've got."

> Things are back to where they were. We're all in our routines. She [the patient] is back at school, playing the flute and soccer. The boys are playing too and going to scouts.

Understandably, families want things to be as they were before CF intruded into their lives, or at least as they are at present, now that the patient has recovered from the excerbation. They renew their efforts to define their situation in relation to normal life. They want to be like and to look like other families. And to a large extent they can, depending on the way they handle the situation. As one mother explained:

> Sure she needs treatments, but we make them, so no one else sees them. We schedule clinic visits around school vacations and holidays. That way, she's not missing school and no one has to know why she is out. Even hospitalizations, especially tune-ups, can be managed with the right schedules. And the extras we give her, the vacations, we just explain as the way we do things now.

Toward the end of the third period, the sixth strategy begins to emerge—*reassessment of family priorities*. The reassessment of family priorities means prioritizing what was once an issue that could be deferred. After their child is diagnosed, many parents talk about the need to get their "priorities in order," "to live every moment as if it were the last," "do it now, not put it off." They tend not to act upon that philosophy, however, until the number of exacerbations and hospitalizations begins to increase. Parents feel it important to make efforts to "spend more time together as a family." It is not unusual, for example, to see families taking more vacations at this time than they had before the child was diagnosed or even in the years immediately following diagnosis.

Period IV—Increased Complications

In the fourth period, the arbitrary and capricious character of CF begins to show itself. Patients become sick more frequently and with less warning. As many patients say:

> You never know when you are going to get sick and have to come in.

Home tutoring is often required at this stage and children frequently are unable to complete school. Complications such as shortness of breath, diabetes, need for medications impinge on patients', parents' and siblings' activities. Oxygen is sometimes needed. The use of oxygen is a highly charged issue for many families. Siblings and parents often refer to the use of oxygen as a "turning point."

In short, in the fourth period, it is far more difficult for families to contain the intrusion CF makes into their lives. Yet they do try. For example, some try to deal with the intrusions hospitalization makes through increased home treatment and home IV therapy. As the 14-year-old well sister of a 13-year-old patient explained:

> Home IV therapy [takes] a lot of time and work, but it's better than the hospital. Then [during home IV therapy] at least we can be home, be a family like other families, have dinner together, watch what we want to watch on TV.

For home IV therapy and all the other chores that go along with it (e.g., chest physiotherapy) to become part of a normal day seems almost a contradiction in terms. But for many, normal has a great deal to do with control—more specifically control of everyday life and home IV therapy offers a way to achieve that.

In this period of increased complications, families continue to strive for control, however elusive and the strategies are means to those ends. Strategies used in the previous periods are still in evidence; however, since the circumstances to which they were directed have changed, the way they are used become somewhat different. Families continue to try to integrate the tasks of CF care into everyday life, but still maintain some kind of normalcy to their existence. This, however, proves to be almost impossible and more often than not leads to cutting back on treatments.

> There is just so much to do. We just can't seem to do it all and have any kind of normal life—so we skip some treatments. At least that way, we do the others. Otherwise, it's too much and we wind up doing nothing. And any way, I'm not sure the treatments do all that much.

Also, the difficulty in getting the patient to comply with treatment contributes to and multiplies cutbacks. By this point, the majority of patients are adolescents or pre-adolescents and don't want to continue with the treatments.

As families and patients endure CF for long periods of time and as they process and sort information about the disease, there is less and less that can be kept from their day-to-day thinking. Information about the prognosis, so neatly tucked away in the back of their minds (the second period), edges forward.

> Every time I go to the hospital, I think this time could be . . . well, you know.

A new view of the future is also projected. While a future still exists, it is diminished. Parents and well siblings speak of the patient as needing to adjust their plans for the future; in terms of career goals it should be something that they will have time to achieve, and regarding their personal life, that they might not being able to have children.

There is a further reassessment of priorities. For well siblings, this translates as: "The patient gets what he wants, while we either have to wait or go without." As one mother of two CF patients and four well children said when talking about the cars she bought for the older patient:

> I give to the kids [referring to the CF patients] more now, maybe more than I should. It spoils them, but really, what difference does it make? It's not like they are going to buy cars when they are older. They may not be able to. I'm not sure that the others [well siblings] think of my doing this. I guess they're jealous, but that's it. It's easier for them to earn money.

The fourth period is a pivotal period in well siblings' acquisition of information about CF and in their relationships with their brothers and sisters. It is at this time that the siblings finally realize that CF is an incurable and uncontrollable disease. As one well brother said of his sister:

> I know they're not going to find a cure and with the lungs filling up, you die. Everybody never makes it. All of her friends die.

Not all well siblings internalize this view of imminent death their dying brothers and sisters. For some well siblings it is not until the sixth period that the terminal prognosis is fully recognized and realized.

Like their parents, when faced with knowledge of the true prognosis of death, many well siblings compartmentalize this information and bury it deep inside, keeping it from their immediate awareness; not all succeed at this. As several siblings remarked to me, "I think about it all the time." They cannot successfully compartmentalize, or put away the information for by this time, the inevitable death is too prominent.

Regardless of their view of the disease and the patient's imminent condition, well siblings are reluctant to discuss their views with the patient and their parents. This, too, is not surprising. Recall that in an effort to keep CF from impinging on their thoughts, parents often avoid discussion of CF—an approach that is interpreted by siblings as a cue not to speak to the patient or their parents about the patient's condition. Also, like their parents, well siblings are concerned not only about the patient's reaction to a frank discussion of the patient's condition, but it is upsetting to them, too.

> I don't want to tell [what I know] because I don't know what is going to happen. I don't know how she is going to react, I don't know if she's just going to say, 'Well, when it happens,' or if she's going to start crying or something like that.

> I don't think I'd be able to talk about . . . to talk about it. I might say something that would get her mad or upset. I'm really scared about what her reactions will be. Maybe something would come up that my parents don't want her to know.

A reluctance to speak is often with full recognition that the patient not only knows about the prognosis but also knows that people are not willing to talk about it. As one healthy sister commented:

> I think she sort of feels out in the cold about [the fact] that we know more about it than what we're telling her. I think she knows—from the people that we have known who have had CF and died. We haven't said that kid had cystic fibrosis, or anything like that. We sort of say it's a shame and leave it at that. We can't really tell her. But she knew one [patient] and that he had treatments like her.

Ironically, if at this point siblings do not share information, a distance is created in the relationship that can last until the patient's death.

> We [referring to the speaker, a well sister and patient] didn't talk. We weren't that close. My sister [another well sister in the family] did talk to Max—they were close.

Once well siblings see CF as a demanding, debilitating and incurable disease, it becomes difficult for them to continue their attempt to have other people see the patient as a person, just like anyone else. Well siblings have difficulty—feeling perhaps less justified—making some of the demands of their parents that they had made earlier. This conversation between the author, a mother and her well son, Randy, illustrates:

Mom: "I want to give Randy more attention. He needs it. He wants to show it, but he can't. He should. It's hard."

Randy: "It's hard for me. What? I should what?"

Mom: "You feel like more—you want some of the attention."

Randy: "No. I don't want most of—I know Ellen has cystic fibrosis and she needs most of the attention.

While well siblings may feel less justified in making their demands known in words, this does not mean that they do not make their needs known in other ways. For example, some well brothers act out in school and others gain weight. It is also not unusual to find well siblings worrying about the patient, becoming more protective of the patient, or even eulogizing and idealizing the patient. These feelings are contained in this well sister's description of her brother, who needed a great deal of care and was often difficult and demanding.

Mom and Dad spend a lot of time with Mel. He's a super brother and he's always sharing things with me. He never thinks of himself only. [Crying, she continues.] Like if he went somewhere and someone was going to give him something, he'd say, 'Can I have another for my sister?' The other day, Mom got him these pizzas, there's two pizzas that come in a box, and she told me I'm supposed to make both of them for me—ahh, for him. He's supposed to eat a lot, you know, and he said, 'You know, Tracy, I won't—I can eat both of them, but I want to share them with you.' You know, that really meant a lot to me. I really don't think you can ask for a better brother.

The well siblings are struggling with thoughts, fears, and concerns that are not so easily managed.

Period V—Increased Deterioration

While the patient's deterioration has been evident for some time (e.g., activities are increasingly limited, oxygen is used more regularly), the fifth period comes when the physician discloses that the patient's condition has become more severe. The disease and the accommodations one must make to it become more a focus of the family's thoughts and everyday life. Like the fourth period (increased complications), the fifth period can last for some time.

As deterioration progresses, three of the strategies families had previously used to meet the challenges of the disease are no longer in evidence. Compartmentalization of information is no longer seen. There is nothing left to push to the back of their minds. The prognosis is clear. As well, no longer do parents or siblings feel that they can maintain any distance from the patient's disease. "Where can we go? How can we escape? It is everywhere." Avoidance of reminders of CF is no longer possible, let alone tenable. Gone are the redefinitions of what is normal. The realm of normal cannot be extended to accommodate the changes that have now taken place. "What is left that's normal? Even the hospital is not normal any-more (in the sense of not being what we were used to)." Nothing can be made to appear normal again.

The other three strategies that address the changes that have taken place in the patient's care and condition remain. For exam-ple, routines for care are now organized around the ever-present catheter and oxygen equipment. The future is now conceived in a radically different way—it is limited to the next months, or even weeks. As one mother put it:

> Now I really know what it means to live one day at a time. I have to, so I can go on and give him what he needs.

There is also a reassessment of priorities. The patient's needs come first: "When he calls, I come. I drop whatever I'm doing. To hell with everyone and everything else." Families endeavor to do what needs to be done which, although they know that by this point it has become a losing battle, it is still a battle they will continue to fight. As one mother said:

> When he asked me, 'Am I going to die this time?' I told him that he didn't have to, but he needed to fight.

Period VI—Death of the Patient

The sixth period follows the family's meeting with the physician about their sick child's prognosis, not just their own observations of changes in the patient's condition. This meeting, referred to by staff as the "Come to Jesus Meeting," is well known to parents at the end-stages of the disease. For example, one mother, looking down the hall at another mother going off to the meeting accompa-nied by the social worker and nurse practitioner, remarked to me:

> When they come for me, I'm not going. I'll know [meaning I'll know what they have to say] by their coming.

For brief and fleeting moments, parents and well siblings think about life without the patient. It becomes "just a matter of time." The strategies that families use to contain the intrusions CF makes into their lives are no longer in evidence. The ultimate intrusion has come—death—and that cannot be contained.

The coping mechanisms families previously used to meet the challenges of living with the CF child are replaced by strategies to meet the challenges of dying. The previously discussed six strategies have served their purpose. As one mother explained:

> What is there left to do? I think he had a normal life, as much as you can have a normal life with CF. Why, right up to the end he was outside there with his brothers—the oxygen in his wagon.

CONCLUSION

Families deal with cystic fibrosis by containing the intrusions it makes into their lives for as long as possible. Family members endeavor to preserve as much of their previous normal way of life, as well as their ideas of a normal life, for as long as possible.

The strategies I have described in this chapter allow families to live, at least for long periods of time, with some modicum of normalcy, some level of control. But it is also clear that by adopting these strategies families are picking up a double-edged sword. For example, while the avoidance of reminders of CF may help parents to go on with other areas of a patient's life that need attention, the adoption of this strategy also creates an atmosphere that well siblings interpret as a directive not to speak. And as I have also noted, when siblings fail to discuss the prognosis, a distance is created in the relationship that can last until death.

Similarly, in the early stages of the disease, the reassessment of family priorities allows families to do what they might not ordinarily do (if, for example, they did not have a child with CF)—like taking family vacations. In the later stages of the illness, this same strategy (however necessary) can lead to the unequal distribution of love and/or the giving of material objects to the healthy children in the family. This is a consequence that well siblings are often reluctant to point out directly, but can come up indirectly in such ways as poor school performance and weight gain. Well siblings have conflicting feelings and concerns; they are torn by feelings of jealousy, guilt, loss and grief.

> She gets treated better because she doesn't have as much of a life. She's gonna die young.

The gifts don't make up for the hurts and other things inside of me. It doesn't make anything. You know, you may smile on the outside, but inside it hurts.

Please note that I am not advocating these strategies; nor am I criticizing them. I am merely documenting them and encouraging families to consider their impact—the pros and the cons—on each family member over the course of the illness.

The development of these strategies is not premeditated, conscious, or even necessarily deliberate. The strategies emerge in everyday life in response to the care the disease requires as well as the thoughts, feelings, and concerns the patient's condition and particular experiences engender.

With advances in CF care and research, CF patients and their families will be able to enjoy relatively normal lives for much longer periods of time. Even now, as in so many other chronic life-threatening illnesses, it is not unusual to find well siblings growing up and leaving home before the disease begins to take its toll. For them, growing up with a brother or sister with CF will have a far different impact than it did on those who grew up with a brother or sister who became severely ill and died in their developmental years.

5

Helping Caregivers who Deal with Dying and Bereaved Children

Thomas Frantz, PhD

Death has—and always will—run counter to our belief in the "American way of life"; with a little hard work and ingenuity there is nothing we cannot accomplish and no problem we cannot solve. Furthermore, in America we have specialists who are able to right things that go wrong; technology is so far advanced today, it seems that very few problems that cannot be overcome. The fact of death is, then, understandably an issue that interferes with our belief that we are masters of all things. There is nothing that can be done to "fix" death—no one to call, no one to "make it better," indeed, no one can change death at all.

As caregivers—in this case, of dying children—we are the people most likely to be present when death occurs. What is the best way for us to act? What should we do? What *can* we do? One of the main things that will help make a difference for the patients, their families, and also for other staff members is simply to *be there*. Willingness to be present—not to run away from the disaster—with the dying child and his or her family during this agonizing time is, in itself, probably the most helpful measure that we as caregivers can offer. Even though we cannot change destiny and cannot make the pain disappear—we can't stop the death—being there provides more help and comfort than one might ordinarily imagine. It is, in fact, perhaps the very best thing we can do.

When a death is occurring, there is a very real transfer of energy that takes place between the people present. This energy transfer is called *entrainment*. Entrainment is analogous to two tuning forks that are set to vibrate at different rates; bring them close together and after a while they will begin to vibrate at the same rate—they entrain and affect each other. Human beings do that too. It is more subtle and harder to see, but it happens all the time and is a very important phenomenon in human interaction. The vibrations that we project affect each other in very meaningful ways. Of course, you have to be open to these feelings in order to feel them. If you are caught up in your own thing and you are not receptive to the energy coming from the people around you, you will most likely miss their vibrations.

If we as caregivers can convey a peaceful energy, a love energy that is very strong and powerful, to those who are dying or bereaved, we will be doing a lot by our presence alone. We will be doing something many people are afraid to do—to be present during someone else's intense pain and grief, to be in the presence of someone who is dying or someone who has just lost his or her child.

A child's death is especially difficult to cope with, even if you have known that child for only a short time. We all feel grief and sadness when we lose someone that we've been taking care of, particularly if that person was a child. In addition, something happens that is highly disconcerting; many people think that a child's death is out of order—it is unnatural, not supposed to happen. Children are supposed to outlive adults.

A man came to a meeting of Compassionate Friends (a group composed of those who have suffered the loss of a loved one) about seven years ago. His son had been hit by a car and killed in August. The meeting took place in October. He said,

> You know, my wife and I were sitting on our back patio drinking iced tea on an August night like we had done many times before, and our son was over at a neighbor's playing. He was supposed to be home at 8:30. At 8:45 he still wasn't home. I got up to go call the neighbor to find out where he was when the phone rang. It was the hospital asking if we had a son named—? They asked if we could go to the hospital right away; there had been an accident. When we got there they told us our son was dead.
>
> I had been sitting there on my patio, minding my own business and not doing any harm to anyone. Then, all of a sudden, from out of nowhere a force swoops down, picks up my son, kills him, takes him away, and I never see him again. If that can happen, anything can happen. As I am sitting here tonight talking to you, how do I know my house is not burning down? How do I know my wife will not be diagnosed with cancer tomorrow? How do I know my little girl is going to be all right? Can you tell me? Can you promise me nothing like this will ever happen again?

Once the unthinkable happens—something that is unnatural—it is hard to have trust in anything for a while and to know where to put our faith. Is there any solid ground on which to put our feet? Is anything for sure? Sometimes our belief that God is all-knowing and all-powerful gets cast aside because of a crisis like this. When a child's death occurs, it pulls the rug out from under us. In addition to our grief and sadness, we may have a crisis of trust and belief. It can make our life extremely uncomfortable and tense.

It seems that when any loss occurs—at that instant when we become aware of the loss—it feels like someone has taken a needle and injected us with a huge dose of an active ingredient—grief. This grief starts to permeate our system, affecting us for as long as it remains within us. The parents of the child get the biggest dose of grief. It will affect them for three to four years, at least. Even those who have had only brief encounters with the child will get their share of grief.

After a certain period of time, even professionals who have been caring for the dying child may become hardened because they can no longer take the pain that builds up after repeated losses. This pool of pain can become so big that after many deaths and losses—especially when caregivers have not learned ways of purging themselves of each new loss—any additional loss can be the straw that breaks the camel's back. The physician who may have been a very caring person at one time may now reach a point where instead of treating Sammy in Room 402, he treats the lymphoma in Room 402. He just cannot deal with the humanness of people anymore. He begins to turn off and become cold. The only way that we, as caregivers can continue to do this work is to find ways of grieving and of syphoning off the pain.

In order to cope with a child's death while at the same time attending to our own needs, it is essential to begin the task of grief release at the *moment of death*. By talking with parents over the years whose children have died for various reasons and in various settings, I have come to the conclusion that the type of response that helps them the most is the same response that helps us the most, too. For example, a nurse came to a workshop that we were conducting. At the end of the workshop she raised her hand and said,

> I just got transferred to a new unit. I have only been there three weeks, but there are infants on this unit and some of them are going to die. Last week, my first baby died. The mother had been keeping a vigil over her dying child, but when he actually died, she was in the cafeteria getting something to eat. My supervisor was gone. I realized that I would have to deal with this alone.

The nurse explained that when she saw the child's mother getting off the elevator, she realized that she would have to tell her that her baby had died. It was not a total shock because the baby was fairly ill, but as the mother came closer and closer, the nurse had no idea what to say. The next thing she remembered was crying on the mother's shoulder, outside the baby's room. The nurse's question at the workshop was, "How can I learn to be more professional? What is my supervisor going to think if she sees me crying and holding the mother in the corridor?" When we talked to the mother some months later about this, she said, "Of all the things that happened when my baby died, the thing I remember most is the nurse who cried with me outside my baby's room."

The most helpful thing to do for the family whose child is dying or has died is to respond in a way that shows that you, too, are affected by what is happening, that you are touched and moved, and that you are not just a professional doing your job. It is extremely helpful for survivors of loved ones to show that the crisis that has just occurred is not just "another death"—it is the Death of Their Child and it hurts staff as much as it hurts the parents.

Death is a time to stop. Something important, something irreversible, has happened. There is no question that "no man is an island" and we are all in this together. It helps if we allow death to affect us naturally, as opposed to "professionally"—presuming that we as caregivers have appropriate feelings of empathy for others' grief.

Most of the time we will not grieve to the extent that the family of the dying or dead child will, but it is essential for us as caregivers to acknowledge our own grief as well as that of our co-workers and to find ways of releasing it. We need to take care of each other in our times of grief, and I find that talking has proven to be the best, if not the simplest, method of confronting grief. The most beneficial people to talk to are your co-workers because they have first-hand knowledge of the situation and will understand what you are going through better than anyone else. It is hard to take your grief home and to talk about it to your family. While they care for you and may understand your pain, they are not as close to the problem as your colleagues are and, therefore, cannot be as helpful.

One of the worst things to do to grieving colleagues is to give them advice. They need a chance to get their feelings out and this must be done in their own way. Maybe they feel guilty because they think they "could have done more." Maybe they need to cry. Sometimes, when someone starts to talk, cry, or express feelings of guilt, it makes us feel uncomfortable and we try to stop them. It isn't hard to see that this is completely unhelpful; the best thing to do is to listen and let them purge their grief. Obviously, we won't have an "answer" for death and we can't "fix" it, but we can *be there*. We need to be there—on the unit, in the counseling agency, or in the church.

It is hard to organize any formal mechanism for grieving and support in a professional setting. It always sounds like a good idea, but scheduling, time, and other duties usually interfere with an ongoing grief/stress support meeting. As a result, informal ways of dealing with grief and stress are the most practical methods.

Grieving may be done in other ways as well. Exercise is a good way of grieving, as is painting and listening to or playing music. When participating in non-oral, non-verbal ways of grieving (such as exercise, painting, sculpture and sports), it isn't just the activity that facilitates grieving, it is also what's on your mind at the time you're engaged in it.

In times of crisis, people do not change their ways of coping and grieving. Most everyone has had a whole lifetime of losses and subsequently, each time there was a loss, from the time we were little, we have somehow reacted, responded, and managed. In the process we have built up our own personal ways of coping and responding to death and loss. For some of us, the ways we adopted worked well; for others, perhaps they didn't work as well. But even those of us who have developed poor ways of grieving are not likely to change at the time of a new crisis. In times of crisis, people frequently regress, reverting to earlier times and their earlier ways of grieving. The more difficult the loss and the more deeply the loss affects them, the more people tend to regress. Shock due to death is so great that it is a bad time to learn new ways of coping. This, therefore, puts a very high premium on the acceptance of other people, because this is a time when their help can be very valuable.

There are some people who have never learned how to grieve. They carry their grief with them long after the loss occurred. They have entered a kind of "seasonless world" because of their fear of the strong feelings within them coming out. The way we humans are made, there is one channel, one conduit, out of which our feelings flow. When in our fear we clog up that channel because we can't face the painful feelings—they are too embarrassing and over-whelming—then the good feelings can't get out either. When some-thing good happens, we don't feel it because the channel is clogged with the fear of those other sad, hurtful feelings coming out. The spark goes out of life. We get by, but the enthusiasm is gone. This is perhaps the price we pay for not knowing how to grieve.

One of the things I have noticed when working with caregivers is that sometimes the deaths of people we work with are not the biggest problem. Work issues, scheduling, getting along with co-workers, and our relationship with our supervisor are of major importance. We need to find ways of releasing the work tensions so that resentments do not build to the point where bad relationships with co-workers and supervisors result.

CHARACTERISTICS OF CAREGIVERS
WITH LONG-TERM SERVICE

1. We are people who like deep relationships with people. We are not satisfied with just surface relationships. We find a lot of meaning in those relationships. We who work with people who are dying are very fortunate in a way because we have the dying as teachers and we are constantly reminded that life, like so many other things, follows the law of supply and demand. When we have all the time in the world, no one day is particularly special. But when days are limited, each day becomes very important. This is one of the main benefits that we can reap from the work we do. We can be continually reminded that life is important and precious and does not go on forever. Dying people also teach us that "when the time of our particular sunset comes, our possessions, our accomplishments, won't really matter a great deal, but the clarity and care with which we have loved others will speak with vitality of the greatest gift of life we've been for each other."

2. We are not in it for the money. People who work with those who are dying are not motivated primarily by money. We are people whose values are oriented more toward the human side than the material side.

3. We are people whose work is not just a job, but rather a part of our life and something we are committed to. We believe in what we are doing, and caring for people in pain is in our blood. In one form or another, we would likely do it whether it was our job or not.

4. The way we cope, aside from catharsis and grieving, is, in effect, by living in the moment. The more you stay in the moment, the more you can focus on what you are doing. When we are at work we really care about the people there; it is not just a job, and we are not in it simply for the money.

We really put ourselves into our work. There is a great benefit to learning to put all your energy fully into what you are doing.

5. We have a broad sense of humor. We have an uncanny ability to find humor in things that other people might find morbid. We are able to laugh. This is a wonderful thing because laughter, in a general sense, is a form of grieving. It is a healing release of energy. Caregivers who are able to stay on the job the longest are those who have found ways to find humor in things.

6. We are assertive and somewhat independent. We do not always go along with what we're supposed to do. We sometimes make waves. We seldom feel like victims. We often take charge and try to maintain control to some extent. This assertiveness and independence is a way of life and is characteristic of people who are rarely sick or defeated.

7. We have the ability to grieve. We have found ways of releasing the energy with which we've been injected. We don't carry the burden of grief around with us for long.

8. Many people who work with dying children feel a little special. Not everyone can do this work; nor can everyone remain long in the presence of pain and death. Not everyone can take care of people who are dying; nor can everyone go into homes and talk with families about losing their loved ones. It is a special talent, and once in a while patting ourselves on the back is appropriate.

Those who are able to put their energies into living cope the best and are able to do this work a lot longer. We are continually reminded of the value of living in the moment and appreciating what is real by doing this kind of work.

I am reminded of a woman who was in the cancer research hospital in Buffalo. On a rainy, overcast November afternoon, I went to see her. She looked up at the ceiling of her room and said, "This is the last ceiling I am ever going to see. I am never going to leave this room alive. It would mean the world to me if I could just go outside and around the block, maybe even in a wheel chair. I know it is damp out and cold, but that would be the most wonderful thing I could think of." I thought to myself, Here I am complaining about the weather, and to her it would be the most wonderful thing imaginable.

Some days we get caught up in the rat race and can not think about much else, but on certain days when I am driving home from work, I think about death over my left shoulder and I ask myself, Who am I not straight with? Who am I upset with? Who do I have unfinished business with? Who do I need to talk with to feel peaceful? By the time I get home, I know who I need to call or who I need to write, or who I need to see the next day. We cannot fix everything, but I think that stopping, pausing, and reflecting about our unfinished business and acting on it is a gift that dying people can teach us.

Another exercise that I recommend is to pause for a moment before you begin a routine, ordinary activity and say to yourself, "Suppose this were the last time I could ever do this." With that thought in mind, go ahead and drive to work as if it were for the last time. You will begin to notice things that you have never noticed before. You will pay more attention and be more aware. Think about putting your children to bed. They never want to go to bed; it is getting late and they want a glass of water and a story, while you are looking forward to some time by yourself. You come to dread bedtime. Some night, just before you put the children to bed, say to yourself, "Suppose this were the last time I will ever put my daughter to bed." Keep that thought in your mind as you tuck her in. My hunch is that you will pay more attention to her, read her that story, look in her eyes, and it will not be quite so important to get it over, because these are moments of life that are very important. If you really were dying and if this were the last time, you would cherish these moments beyond measure.

Stopping from time to time is a very good way of taking care of ourselves. You can benefit by stopping at certain times, such as before you get out of your car to go into the house, just stopping for 30 seconds and tuning into yourself and thinking about what is important. These little pauses in life can be points where we gather our energy and get in touch with our priorities. A few minutes between clients can make a very big difference because in those minutes you can become aware, and I think awareness is one of the major things that makes us human. You cannot change things that you are not aware of. Awareness is the first step toward any kind of change and it is of the essence of humanity to make choices. Dead people do not make choices; rocks do not make choices. Living human beings make choices.

6

Doing and Integrating: Holism for Caregivers

Rick Kelly, CCW

In considering the topic of the care of caregivers, I had to reflect on the exact nature and purpose of my talking to and with others who are very actively involved in similar endeavors. I certainly do not want to be in the position of bringing coals to Newcastle, but I do want to contribute in some constructive and positive manner. In this chapter I would like to discuss my own experiences with the hope that they will intertwine with those of my readers.

My comments are based on my experiences as a mental health consultant at the Hospital for Sick Children in Toronto, where my primary focus is nursing. It is important to understand that I am speaking from an experiential point of view, not from a research perspective. Therefore, I am more concerned with individual meanings and construction of events as they pertain to one person or group of persons caring for another person. In this case, I am referring specifically to a child who is going to die. I am concerned with the psychological dimension for the caregiver as he or she encounters the events and processes involved in a situation such as this. Although some of what I have to say will bear on the stress dimension of caring for the terminally ill child, I am more concerned with tracking down the individual importance and impact that caring for the dying child in this context carries with it. That is what led me to title this chapter as I did. When I thought of "doing and integrating," I was thinking of how one can actively be in such caregiving situations and what its components are, while at the same time maintaining a sense of (for lack of a better phrase) psychic wholeness.

My last comment has to do with the role and function of symbolization in our construction of the particular shape and form of events that surround us. I am borrowing this concept from Robert Jay Lifton's work on the psychology of extreme conditions (probably making enough of my own recommendations to render his meaning unrecognizable).

Symbolization, whether we talk of it in terms of images or forms, is the way in which we represent the world to ourselves, internally and externally. The images that come out of our symbol-making also become reference points and guides to our own inner experiences—hopefully not definitive, but certainly carrying substantial psychic weight.

It is very common that the event of death is seen from the caregiver's point of view as a type of stress. Therefore, our understanding is directed to defining the stress, identifying the symptoms and establishing effective coping strategies. While I am not suggesting that this way of constructing the caregiver's experience does not have some decided benefits, it is also important to stand back and look at some of the implications. First, when I reflect on stress and its ancillary concepts, my sense is that we have moved into the realm of our own predominant death culture whose primary focus is to deny, conquer, master and otherwise sanitize our lives of the presence of death. What else is coping all about? Second, if stress is the perspective from which we talk about death and its implications, even if it is in the context of work, then we are all in danger of no longer being able to lay claim to both larger and personal meanings that cannot be captured in a stress framework.

So it is from this point of view that I want to discuss the range of symbols, images and forms that are used in the conceptual framework that bounds our talking of death from a caregiving point of view. Ultimately, stress management resides in each individual's opportunity and ability to articulate an inner sense of meaning in such a way that it maintains and reinforces both an intra- and interpersonal connectedness; this also, is the ultimate integrity.

FOUR MAPS

Map 1

What I want to do is to discuss four maps. The first map tells us where we are—the name of the place. Suppose that we rename the place and no longer refer to it solely or primarily as a "stressful event," but that we refer to the place as "meaning." If we reflect on some of the important events that have led to our consideration of death and subsequent grief, one of the intellectual markers that has allowed all of us to give death and dying its due respect was George Engel's concept of grief. The bald summary of his thoughts is that grief is real and that there are real consequences depending on the way in which we choose, or are able, to engage in the grieving process. We are very adept at applying the concept when we approach children and families; we appreciate grief as real and also unique and see it as part of a necessary process. More and more we are plumbing the subtleties and nuances of these processes in order to understand them better. Yet when it comes to caregivers, we have not reached the level of understanding that we have with families and children. Our ways of understanding death for a caregiver is generally a stressful situation. We do not have ways of sufficiently understanding and acknowledging the meanings that accord the caregiver the dignity and respect that should both precede and follow the experience of the death of a child in the context of his or her caregiving. If our understanding is limited, then surely it is not difficult to imagine the low level of sophistication in which our practical supports exist.

There is no question that the grief caregivers experience over the death of a child is real; although it may not be real in the same way as it is for parents, this difference does not diminish the grief; it does emphasize the unique and individual meanings death has for each person involved. Therefore, by accepting the fact that grief is indeed an undeniable reaction to death for caregivers, then it is also necessary to accept the other things that we have learned about grief: grief entails both an emotional and instrumental process; and unresolved grief has a number of implications, one of which is that it makes it difficult for survivors to "risk" forming significant attachments to other people again because they fear the possibility of experiencing another loss when or if that person dies.

The study of bereavement has shown us that there are different parameters that seem to have significance for the way in which people construct and attribute different meanings to the death event. Weisman suggests that death can be viewed from a "timely" and an "untimely" the point of view. Death is generally considered to be timely when survival equals expected survival, and untimely when it is seen as premature, unexpected or calamitous. If one applies this to those individuals who care for terminally ill children, all deaths obviously cannot be considered premature; in many situations the deaths are unexpected or calamitous, or both.

During a session I was conducting on how children view death, I was commenting that children primarily see death as unfair. "But isn't that true?" a nurse asked me. Therefore, the meaning that a caregiver will place on the death of children who have suffered some form of physical assault by an adult will be significantly different than the meaning they place on the death of children who have outlived their projected life expectancy and experienced a loss in the quality of their lives. My experience is that in the first instance grief is often expressed in the form of ruminating on and questioning the incomprehensibility and unfairness of the death itself; any form of reason is rarely achieved. In the latter instance I have often heard it expressed that the death has a dimension of disguised blessing and subsequently people are able to express both positive and sad feelings, and allowing time for remembrance of the child who has died. As well, because of being able to view the death in a positive light, people do not tend to fall into the rut of not wanting to establish new relationships.

Bugen has developed a model of human grief that asserts that the degree of grief is best predicted and measured by the degree of the closeness of the relationship and the caregivers' perception of the degree to which they feel they can prevent the child's death. Closeness of relationship is a common development for caregivers; relationships will develop with children of any age, from neonates to teenagers. This element affects the process of bereavement in a specific way: if the relationship is important at the time of death, grief will tend to be more intense and the relationship must be pushed into a peripheral position in order for grief to be resolved. The closeness that inevitably forms between the sick child and the caregiver creates various problems: caregivers who rearrange their schedules and vacations in order to be available to the child who is seriously ill; caregivers who request that they be assigned to the child each time they are on duty; and those who are worried that the child may die if they are not always on their shift. However, those who do not have a particularly close relationship with the sick child will have a milder reaction to the child's death. This in itself accounts for the wide range of responses that are often seen in a team of caregivers; a range that extends from intense emotion to moderate reactions.

The concept of the caregiver's ability to prevent a child's death is in direct relation to the belief in the degree of preventability they believe they had in relation to the actual death and the level of responsibility they had in contributing to this death. What is important to note is the word "belief." I have often sat with individuals who have seriously questioned themselves from the point of view of "What if I had only . . . ?" It is natural to question oneself and one's contributions, but some individuals are dogged by a persistent sense of responsibility that has subsequent effects regarding their future relating to children.

Therefore Map 1 moves us away from a generic name for the land as "stress" and toward the name "meaning," which should enable us to develop a true phenomenology of these multivariate experiences. That is why I chose to utilize some of our understanding of death and grief with respect to other individuals and contexts, in order to tickle our imagination with other ways of looking at the meaning of some caregiving experiences. Also it should allow us to positively connote what it is that is being described.

Map 2

Map 2 has to do with the things that caregivers bump into in this land; metaphorically, one could call them rocks; practically, they are the real events that are problematic and the inner experiences that are evoked by such events. I have been able to identify four rocks by both what is said to be and by what I have observed myself. There are likely many more rocks that I have not seen. Let me show you some of these rocks and the faces they wear.

ROCK 1

Rock 1 is characterized by questions such as the following:

> What do I say if he asks me if he is going to die?
> What do I say if he asks me what happens after he dies? What do I do if he tells me what he thinks it is like after he dies?
> What if he says he is going to be with the rest of his family afterwards? This kid is turning into a real handful . . . but I don't want to be harsh or punitive given what he is going through. How can I set reasonable expectations?
> What can I do for this child who is dying?
> How do I deal with these parents who are so critical of us but don't seem interested in any other alternatives?
> What do we do with these parents who are refusing to accept the child's eminent death and won't even consider removing life supports?
> What do I say when they say that they are going to be taking this to their lawyer?

How can I be sure that we've done everything to make sure that they are ready to take their child home? That they are not going to have second thoughts? That they are not going to have a major sense of guilt when their child dies at home?

ROCK 2

Rock 2 is known more by the shadow it casts than by anything that is directly observed. At the same time it has a strong tendency to appear wherever Rock 1 is. In fact this rock could be said to be the map that directs the questions in Rock 1. Rock 1 concerns itself with the "how to do" issues. Rock 2 is made up of the knowledge and understanding domain. It consists of such things as the following:

What do children understand of death?
What sort of understanding do they have of their own death and mortality?
What are their needs when facing death (which naturally involves an understanding of normal development)?
What sort of process, what behaviors, what feelings do they experience facing death?
How do families respond to the death of a child? Does it differ according to different factors?
What do families need to make their grief more easily resolved?
What are risk considerations?
What is the role of different cultures in the anticipation of death and subsequent grief?
How do religious perspectives affect the meaning given to death of a child?

I think it is very easy to see how from many of the "what to do" questions one can surmise that another layer of rock formation exists, and that they are very much interrelated like hand and glove. Knowing certain things will direct one's activities; it may not give the specific skill required, but it focuses the energies.

ROCK 3

Rock 3 has to do with the feelings and emotions that caregivers experience in their work with seriously ill and dying children. There were a number of graphic scenes and encounters that led me to discover this rock. The first was a nurse who said, "You know,

I've never had quite this type of feeling before . . . I've worked with a few other children before who have died, but I've never felt this way before." The second encounter was with a group of my favorite nurses who called me to their ward to talk about a well-liked child who had died suddenly and very unexpectedly during what had been considered a relatively minor surgical procedure, at least in comparison to the surgeries she had been through in her life (also note the parameters of unexpectedness of death and closeness of relationship). As we talked about what had happened, it naturally expanded to a remembrance of who she had been as a person. I was profoundly moved by the outpouring of sadness and grief; it was very real and very intense. I said to myself, Where does this get covered in the job description for these people? As I got up to leave, I wondered if I was going to make it out of there under my own steam, so infused was I by the emotion that filled that room. When I think of job descriptions, it reminds me of the regular program we run for almost all new incoming nurses. The morning session is devoted to discussing family-related issues, and the afternoon is devoted to reality shock and stress management. Inevitably, the topic comes up of the deaths that individuals have encountered on the wards. Two elements stand out: it is a time of sadness and frustration, but it is also a shock to many of the nurses who did not expect to find such a prevalence of deaths as part of their job. For other nurses that I have dealt with on other wards, the experience of caring for a dying child evoked feelings of intense anger, frustration, despair, and anxiety, which in a few instances have persisted and led them to call into question their own functioning and coping ability. I wonder about all those who do not feel free enough or are not given the opportunity to express how they are feeling.

ROCK 4

Rock 4 is characterized by the situations that challenge the ethics and values of the caregiver. These situations can arise in relation to the health care system and the way it tends to go about doing its business. But they also arise in the context of attempting to engage with individuals and families at a time when a series of inversions are occurring in their lives: the not-wished-for is happening; their privacy is made public; their normal ways of coping no longer apply; their control over life is given, in large part, to people who are strangers.

Returning to the first set of circumstances, it seems that these ethical challenges have to do with the way in which decisions are made with regard to choices of treatment or non-treatment. Thus, when decisions are made in isolation, or the choice of treatment seems to run counter to alternative perceptions of what is warranted and possible, the sense of ethical isolation increases, along with questions about the right thing to do. Another aspect of this same systems dimension is the difficulty a large, busy, acute-care facility has in switching gears when palliation is required. The challenge in all of this is for caregivers to maintain a consistent focus of caring in the context of medical plans they have not been privy to, or with which they are not in full agreement.

From the family point of view, it is expected that given the level of stress they are going through, they will demonstrate a range of behaviors and choices that can often confuse, if not challenge, the perspective of the caregiver and their own respective set of values. Although it is generally accepted as a professional responsibility that one will honor the autonomy of one's clientele, this principle does not in itself address the impact of a value challenge. Additionally, caregivers must find some degree of peace while rendering their caring in the context of another person's set of values. This often arises in the face of different cultural and religious practices, but it can also occur when one encounters parents who are dealing, for the first time, with the imminent death of their child. Thus there is a rock in this land that is characterized by both systems, treatment content issues and family patterns and choices that can strongly effect the ethics and values of caregivers.

Map 3

Map 3 is the formulation of map 2; it will lead us to understand what all of these different rocks really mean and then allow us to decide what sorts of practical and active responses we need to offer to caregivers.

I would put our rocks into two piles:

Pile 1	*Pile 2*
Skills	Emotions
Knowledge	Ethics

Then I would change them into action words that strike me as having more active significance:

Pile 1	*Pile 2*
Doing	Feeling
Knowing	Valuing

Then I would say that on the left-hand side are elements that represent instrumental needs, and on the right-hand side are elements that represent integrative needs. Let me develop both these items a bit more.

Instrumental needs reflect our concern with doing things in the external world, which I believe is very much in keeping with the central project of caring; it is a demonstrative affair. But doing can also be placed on a continuum that finds at its opposite end helplessness, with a number of midpoints along the way. Also, it is useful to return to the concept of preventability, but with some modification. If the question remains after a discussion or session with the nurse, "Did I do all that I could," this is a cause of concern. Now this is not usually said in the sense of the actual death, but in relation to all the caring that could be provided. Part of the answer to that question ends in ensuring that there are systems and supports in place that allow for and facilitate maximum doing. This type of doing is the kind that allows one to authentically and proudly say, "I did all that I could." We must also remind ourselves that this question has even more attenuated the real limitations of the situation; it is a situation where what is needed most is not able to be given.

Now let me elaborate on my designation of the affective and value needs as being related to an overall sense of integration. (For me the opposite end of the continuum is disintegration, which I mean as a type of psychological intactness or its lack.) The experiences that caregivers encounter in their caring for seriously ill children often involve very powerful emotional and value-laden moments that in their very nature can affect the core of a child's being. However, if no clear recognition is given to these emotions and value challenges at an individual, collegial and institutional level, the tendency is for individuals to engage in a wide range of denying and defending responses. As a result, people engage in distancing themselves from their own real inner experiences. This begins the first level of disintegration; it is an internal fragmentation of experience. It is quite easy to imagine how larger social and organizational systems are not called upon to attend to these real experiences since the experiences themselves, in the most extreme instances, are disowned and belittled by the individuals themselves. Obviously these people are not in any position to advocate for their own needs since the motion of their energies is taking them in a different direction. What also makes this level of need so critical is that the majority of nurses I have worked with clearly identify the fact that they cannot share with their friends or families many of their most important work-related experiences.

The potential for spiraling and compounding situations that contain isolation from oneself and significant others can make for a lethal combination. This is where the phrase "lives of quiet desperation" aptly applies.

It is important to keep in mind that I am using extremes in order to highlight the range of possibilities that can arise; this is not to say that they are the only possibilities. In fact I could very well use as examples instances of excellent caring that reflects the type of integration and connecting to others that is healthy and productive.

Map 4

Map 4 is the one that leads us to where we want to go. It is the map that tells us how to meet the needs of effective doing while maintaining and achieving psychological and social integration. As a result some of the rocks that caregivers stumble across and bump into start to disappear.

I have broken down the interventions and approaches into five categories, four of which I can name and the last can only be described. The preceding four areas are social support, education, organizational practice and research.

SOCIAL SUPPORT

I liken social support to a form of a psychosocial immune system that both buffers and protects the caregiver from the emotional and ethical shocks that are delivered in the process of caring. There is, as well, a meta-message that is sent when support is provided effectively to caregivers. The message is that the way that you are provided for as a caregiver is also the way in which I expect and am supporting you to care for parents and children in distress.

If we accept the idea that the questions of adequacy and accomplishment that arise as part of the grieving process are significant, then forums for group discussion and processing are indicated. These group forums must contain safety, support and permission to express a range of emotions from the positive to what many of us might call the negative. The goals are as follows:

1. To allow caregivers to grieve and mourn.
2. To allow caregivers to validate and reference their own individual contributions.
3. To publicly acknowledge caregivers' experiences and subsequent emotions as an aspect of their work.

4. To facilitate peer support and normalization of emotions.
5. To achieve closure for caregivers through practical planning for caregiver follow-up to the family (funeral attendance, remembrances, flowers).

Being part Irish I benefit from a long-established tradition of wakes; therefore I reduce group forums down to their basics, which have to do with telling stories, laughing and naturally lots of crying. Another form of social support comes about through the establishment of buddy systems and preceptor roles that pair the more experienced and wise with the eager and keen.

If individuals are assured that there are mechanisms in place and others available, then weathering the storms of caring is made much easier. It is certainly easier to be "in it together" than to be "in it alone."

EDUCATION

Returning to the instrumental or doing side of caring for such children and their families, I believe we need to utilize educational input in both a structured and strategic manner so that both the individual and organization benefit.

Death education for professionals needs to reflect adult learning principles as well as a sensitivity to the unique needs generated by such a topic. Approaches that utilize the "whack on the side of the head" technique, which involves shocking caregivers into wakeful alert as they write their own obituary, only induce guilt and a sense of inadequacy. At some level we all appreciate our own mortality; we do not have to wear it on our sleeves.

This education needs to be practical and relevant. It needs to include a focus on the important people skills that are called for at the time of impending death. It needs to incorporate the most up-to-date information and research that we have regarding the topic. It should attend to the needs and feelings of the caregiver. There also should be time for the participants to try on some of the skills, get feedback, make their own conclusions and ultimately integrate their new discoveries.

Time is needed to examine our participation in and contribution to the particular death system and culture in which we find ourselves working. Such an exercise in self-consciousness allows us to acknowledge some of the limitations that surround us. As we deconstruct, hopefully this will lead to the opportunity to co-create and co-evolve another type of death system.

This last approach would, if provided, be the ultimate indicator that we are participating in the co-creation of an alternative death system. This would involve a systematic educational curriculum that addresses all the individuals, not simply the caregivers, who have some contact or knowledge of dying children in their work capacity. This curriculum would also grow and mature along with the individuals and the knowledge that we are able to harvest.

ORGANIZATIONAL PRACTICE

In order to give caregivers practical support in their endeavors to respond to the children we are discussing, clearly defined programmatic aids are needed:

1. Protocols and procedures that outline the phases that one may encounter in the process of caring for the dying child and the family as well as the helpful approaches and suggestions that can be offered or utilized.
2. Clearly spelled-out protocols that address the issues of do-not-resuscitate and withdrawal-of-care orders. Such protocols need to address the substantive issue of determining the choices that can be made as well as the designation of decision-making and inclusion roles (e.g., physician, nurse, parents, child).
3. Areas that deal with children who die need to have a resource bank or library that contains appropriate literature for children and other family members.
4. It is important to have a directory of community resources that can assist the caregiver in directing the parents to supports that can be accessed by them at a later date.

At another level it is important to engage the organization in terms of its own unique language and concerns—quality assurance and staff retention. Quality assurance scrutiny needs to be focussed on the health care practices that occur in relation to the special needs of the dying child. Similarly, one dimension of staff retention is the presence or absence of staff supports that effectively allow professionals to respond to the particularly trying and stressful challenge of caring for such children.

RESEARCH

From the point of view of research, it is important to increase the type of work that is being done in the area of children and dying.

The more we are sensitized to the child's and family's experience, the more our practice will be reflective of this increased understanding. At the same time we will probably become more sensitive to our own experiences through this process of increasing awareness.

Finally, our research efforts need to be directed to a phenomenology of meaning that can both appreciate and represent the structure and the construction of the death event of children for professional caregivers. What is accorded to children and families needs to be given to the caregiver as well.

My last comment has to do with encouraging a certain attitude rather than stating a specific approach to support caregivers. In the search for saving grace we would do well to look at the embodiment of nurturing found in the historical project of women's caring. If we were to pursue this theme and at the same time borrow some ideas developed by such contemporary ethicists as Carol Gilligan and Nel Noddings, they would lead us to look at the uniquely feminine experience that contains within it the fact of a natural, and probably preconscious, attachment and relatedness to others through the process of being born and giving birth. This fundamental attachment and connectedness to others becomes a value and subsequently the foundation for an ethic of caring and responsibility. At what other time in a person's life are her "needs as a stranger" more warranting of an ethic of caring and responsibility for another? At a time of the fundamental disconnecting of human bonds, the profound ethic of caring and connecting is no better placed.

III

The Bereaved Child

7

Children Coping with Death

Sr. Caroline O'Connor, CSJ

As a bereaved sibling myself, it means a great deal to me to be able to write this chapter for children who have experienced the death of a parent, brother or sister, as well as for adults who have not yet worked through their grief over the death of a sibling or parent. It is my hope that readers will be able to benefit from my experiences.

Recently I asked a nurse at our hospital if she was going to a conference on children and death. She said, "No, but I should. When I was 4 years old, my mother and I took my father to the plane and waved good-bye to him, and 3 hours later we got word that the plane he was on had crashed and all the passengers had been killed. Following that, my mother whisked me off to my relatives and I never saw my father again. That was 20 years ago."

Another nurse said, "I should go because I know it would probably help me. When I was 10 years old, my parents and I went to the beach to swim. I clearly remember that bright sunny morning at the beach. I could swim, but when I got caught in an undertow, my father swam over to help me. He saved me, but in the effort he drowned. After this happened, I was sent to stay with my relatives. No one ever talked to me about my father and they certainly never discussed whether his body was ever discovered or even if he was buried. Just before school started in September, my mother came to pick me up. We still did not mention my father's death; we didn't even mention his name. Understandably, I was confused and was carrying a heavy guilt load."

The death of a child must surely be one of the most devastating experiences to be endured by a family. Feelings of sadness, anger, guilt can sometimes be infinitely more destructive than the actual death itself—especially if these feelings persist for long periods of time. Children are simply *not supposed* to die, and few parents are prepared to deal with this tragedy when it does happen.

Bereaved parents assume that children cannot cope with death and so they try to protect them by leaving them out of any discussion. Those of us who have been through this experience of repression know it is a terrible price to pay because it remains unfinished business—unresolved grief—for the rest of our lives.

As a child I experienced a horrible, frightening loss; when I came home from school one day my parents were standing on the verandah and crying. My father said, "Danny is dead." I ran upstairs and found my brother on the bed. I shook him, sat him up and shook him some more. Eventually the undertaker came and took him away, and after a couple hours he brought him back in a small, white coffin. During the wake no one spoke to the three of us children; they must have felt, "I don't know what they would know about it"—meaning, we weren't worth talking to. For whatever reason, our parents were grieving too much to even think about us or our needs at that moment. We were not allowed to attend the funeral. We never let anyone see us crying because "big boys and girls were not supposed to cry." How I longed to reach behind the clouds and bring Danny back. One day I cried out loud in school. My teacher sent me over to the convent for a cookie. The Sister housekeeper gave me a drink and a cookie and asked me to tell her all about Danny. She just listened while I unloaded all my feelings. I knew from her smile that she understood. What a relief it was!

When we deny children the opportunity of mourning, we are pushing them away. We isolate them. They feel absolutely and totally deserted by everyone.

In a family with three children, the 1-year-old brother had died. The two little girls were taken away to stay with friends until after his funeral. When the parents came to pick them up, the children ran away into the fields—they did not want to go home with them.

There is an indescribable sadness in knowing that a child's life is about to end, and anguished parents, faced with this ordeal, often react in ways harmful to the dying child and to the other members of the family. Experience tells us that it is better for parents to be frank with their children about death. Children want to participate and share at a time when they need the warmth and love of their family.

We must communicate honestly and openly with children. Often when children ask questions we can't answer them fully, but we can say to them, "As the days and months go on we'll talk more about it and you'll understand." Don't stifle their questions; let the children see your grief and reassure them that expressions of grief are necessary and normal. Trust their ability to cope.

Schools can also present problems. Sometimes a child may want to keep to herself and the teacher will say, "Isn't it about time you were over this?" when the little girl is just trying to get past the shock. Never put a time limit on grief. The power of grief is so great that it can destroy us, but it also can strengthen us.

One day 10-year-old John was called to the principal's office and was told his brother was killed in a bicycle accident. He also was told it was better his brother had died because he would otherwise have been a vegetable the rest of his life. John said, "I don't care if he'd been a vegetable; I want him with me."

Often reality does not set in immediately after the death of a sibling. Sometimes the young child fantasizes that his brother or sister is just away on a trip. Often a child is told, "Your brother is in heaven. He was so good that God wanted him back." The child becomes afraid that if he is good God will take him back, too. "Will this soon happen to me? Are my parents going to die next? I'll be all alone."

I once asked a couple of boys who had lost a brother to share their experience with the class if they wished. One started to speak and broke down. He said, "It was all my fault my brother died. I killed him. We fought a lot. I made it hard for my mom, too, when she gave him so much attention. I'd like to talk to my mom and dad and brothers and sisters. But they don't want to talk about it very much." I took him out of the room and talked with him. Afterward he came back into class and said, "I just wanted to say that I loved my brother."

Children often feel that thoughts can kill. Communication can help them to realize that this is not so but that thoughts like this are normal. Yet, often in the death of a sibling, brothers and sisters tend to remember the hostile events rather than the loving ones. They forget that it's natural for brothers and sisters to fight. It is just part of growing up. After a death, instead of remembering all the good things we shared or did together, we often think back to the times we shouted at each other.

MEMORIES

For those who have suffered the loss of a brother or sister or parent it is essential that they remember all the good things and the happy times. Put pictures around because the important thing to remember is not that a brother or sister has died but that they lived. That's it exactly. Celebrate memories.

Let the pain out. It takes courage to do this, but it's the only way to recover. There is no easy route through the pain of grief. If parents cut off a child's suffering because they can't stand to see him in pain, they must ask themselves, "Do I want my child to suffer deeply right now or do I want him to suffer quietly and unconsciously for the rest of his life?"

Pain fades to a dull ache. The wound heals but the scar remains forever. We learn to live with the memories, the lost hopes, the shattered dreams. We never get over the death, but we do recover, adjust, and learn to live with it.

RELIGION

Religion can play an important part in our lives. It is a source from which people get a tremendous amount of comfort and a sense of ongoingness beyond life. We frequently see that when the physical powers decline, the spiritual sense increases. Michelle was a 7-year-old girl who grew up in a family where religion had very little part. The morning she died, she jumped out of bed, put her arms around her mother and said, "Mommy, I want to go to God where I won't have any more pain." Andy, an 8-year-old boy, pressed a crucifix in my hand a few hours before he died and said, "I want you to keep this in remembrance of me." Many children are talking to God long before we adults zero in on what they are experiencing.

FUNERALS

Children should be given the opportunity to go to wakes and funerals if they choose. Ask them carefully about their wishes.

Joyce was in kindergarten when her older brother Eric was killed in a motorcycle accident. In spite of my request, she was not allowed to go to the wake. The next week she fainted in church. I saw her fall and knew it was more than a faint. I called her mother and she took Joyce to a doctor who said it was the beginning of petit mal seizures. She experienced the seizure in church because she knew that that was where her brother was just before he was buried.

Four-year-old Cathy was not allowed to see her father in his coffin. A week later her mother and I took her to the cemetery. Before she got in the car, she went to the garage and brought out her red shovel. When her mother asked her what she wanted it for she said, "I am going to dig Daddy up." Instead we gave her flowers to put in a vase and asked her to dig a hole in which the vase could be placed, and she did.

The mother should be given an opportunity to wash her child, to comb her hair, and to put on her clothes with the family present if they wish. In one case where a 3-year-old child put on her little sister's booties, she said to her mother, "Can we take her home now, Mommy?"

The funeral marks with dignity the conclusion of an earthly life, whether it be of 18 months or 80 years. It gives the child in all of us the opportunity to say a last farewell to our loved one.

FINALE

The family that has endured the death of a child has lost a part of itself that can never be replaced, and it has forfeited a stake in the future that will never be realized. It is devastating to be forced to say good-bye to a child whom one is just getting to know and love and whose very existence is based on an inherent faith in the future. Death reveals the incredibly fragile and precious thread upon which life and death are balanced—for facing death is really facing life.

I would like to sum up my thoughts with what might be considered an ideal family in time of crisis.

Jeremy was $8\frac{1}{2}$ years old when he died of cystic fibrosis. He was a very active little boy until about 3 days before he died, when he went into a deep coma. He was unable to talk to anyone about death before this happened. A few days before his death, his mother found the story of "The Flying Horse" in his room. He wanted to let his parents know that he knew death was approaching. The story was full of feelings and symbolism; it ended with his leaving the horse show behind, which was a symbol of "good luck." During his illness, his $4\frac{1}{2}$-year-old brother Justin drew pictures of Jeremy and himself, depicting the very strong feelings of each of them at various stages of Jeremy's last illness. These are now serving as precious memories to the family. A few months after Jeremy died, the family moved out of their city only to find they had made a mistake. They have now returned to the city where they have established a warm, loving and trusting relationship in support of each other.

8

Permission to Grieve: Developing a Children's Grief Support Group

Kathleen Braza, MA

Why would anyone need permission to grieve? Why would a child, or anyone else for that matter, need permission to experience this very natural response to loss?

Children are frequently sheltered from information surrounding the death of a loved one; often in an attempt to "protect" children from pain, we deprive them of the important and necessary opportunity to learn about the dynamics of normal, healthy grief. Because children are treated this way, they often feel alone with their pain, frequently disguising their true feelings of fear, guilt, anger and hurt. Ironically, children often react this way in an attempt to "protect" their parents from worrying about them. Many children carry painful "grief secrets" with them well into their adult years—a result of never confronting the pain they experienced over the death of a loved one when they were children. These problems can include feelings of responsibility for the death, nightmarish images of what their loved one looked like at death and the compounded problems of their personal "unfinished business," which by the time children have reached adulthood has had years and years to fester.

For several years, the Bereavement Program at Holy Cross Hospital in Salt Lake City, Utah, has offered grief support services for children. These groups provide children with the opportunity to experience the pain of loss in a supportive and nonjudgmental environment that accepts the unique ways each child expresses personal grief. Children of all religious and cultural backgrounds are invited to participate.

PROGRAM GOALS AND OBJECTIVES

The children's grief support groups offer bereaved children:

- The opportunity to meet other children who are experiencing the pain of loss.

   Observers during the first night of group often note the surprise on the children's faces when they meet other children who hurt in the same way they do. It is clear that many children have never met other children who have also lost someone they loved.

- Information about normal, healthy grief.

   Many children have no idea that what they are feeling is indeed a normal feeling. Parents who feel as if they must "be strong" in front of their children, often end up only confusing them; children can easily confuse what seems like "no reaction" as "my parents don't even care" or "if I died, Dad would not even cry." The children's grief group not only offers children information about grief, but also encourages them to express it in healthy and appropriate ways.

- Skills for healthy expression of the feelings of grief.

   The children's grief support groups offer children a wide range of tools for the expression of grief. These include stress-management, biofeedback techniques and the very successful use of visual imagery to help children express their pain and complete their unfinished business.

- A safe and supportive environment to express feelings of grief.

   Since children often feel that they must "protect" others from their expressions of pain, it is important to offer children a safe and confidential environment where they are free to release their feelings of hurt and can, if necessary, share their personal "grief secrets".

- Unconditional love and acceptance.

   The success of any grief support group depends in large part on the unconditional love and acceptance of the children by the group leaders. Within this context, it is critical for group facilitators to be in touch with their own fears, attitudes and beliefs (as well as any unresolved grief they may have) that could potentially interfere with unconditional acceptance of the children.

GROUP STRUCTURE

The children's grief support groups are open to children ages 7 to 14 who have experienced the death of a loved one. It is not unusual to have several 7- and 8-year-olds in the same group with 12- and 13-year-old children. Grief is a common bond that seems to bridge the age differences. Occasionally children who are experiencing grief responses that are too painful or have caused them to become entirely dysfunctional will be referred to professionals who can best serve their unique psychological needs. It is emphasized to parents that the groups are educational and supportive in nature and should not be considered "therapy."

Children attend the grief support group for 4 or 5 weeks, depending on the nature of the group. Sessions last for 60 to 90 minutes. Children are invited to attend within 6 weeks or more following their loss experience. We have found that children who have lost a loved one prior to 6 weeks are often in too much pain to feel comfortable sharing in a group experience. Once the group has started, no new children can attend. This helps with group cohesiveness as well as trust-building.

There is no charge for the groups, which are facilitated by two adults who are trained in bereavement as well as group dynamics. Children attend the groups without their parents. We have found that when parents are in attendance, the children feel less comfortable about sharing openly.

Registration forms are filled out by parents prior to the child's participation in the group. These forms include pertinent background information, a description of the loss experience and any parental concerns. A release form regarding hospital liability is also filled out.

The group leaders contact each family after the completion of the group to discuss any concerns and additional ways families can be supportive to the children. Group leaders frequently discuss concerns with parents informally after each group. Children are aware that any personal issues shared with the group will remain confidential and will not be shared with parents without the child's permission. A brief evaluation form is sent to parents and to the children after completion of each group. The hospital bereavement volunteers make follow-up phone calls to each family 3, 6 and 12 months after the child has completed the group.

GROUP OUTLINE

Although group leaders have an "agenda" for each weekly meeting, the unique needs of each group often determine the content of the sessions. For example, children who did not attend a funeral may require special imagery techniques to help them say good-bye to the person who has died.

Week 1

Chairs arranged in a circle comprise the seating arrangement for group one. The children are asked to introduce themselves and to share their own loss experience. The children are usually nervous and self-conscious, so it is important to ask questions frequently to help them tell their "story." These questions may include: When did it happen? How did she die? Were you there when it happened? Did you go to the funeral? These questions often provide group leaders with information that may need to be clarified in future group meetings.

The group leaders also introduce themselves and discuss the purpose of the group, as well as the structure of the group and its rules. It should be emphasized that this is a grief group in which participants will discuss things that will be hurtful and painful at times. It is also important to tell the children that only one person should talk at a time.

Since the children tend to be nervous and ill at ease during this initial session, it is a prime opportunity to discuss the stress that accompanies grief and the various techniques that can be used to manage times of stress. We have discovered that a small biofeedback card is an extremely successful tool for teaching children to relax and to be in control of their stress. This card, entitled "RELAX," has a heat-sensitive square on the front that changes colors as the child becomes more relaxed.* When the children press on the square they will discover that it is black, i.e., an indication of stress. They are then asked to lie on the floor in a relaxed position and listen to a progressive relaxation exercise followed by an imagery story. Stories are taken from several sources (Murdock 1987; Pappa 1982). After listening to the story and once they begin

---

*Additional information on biofeedback "RELAX" cards can be obtained from Stress Management Resources, P.O. Box 9478, Salt Lake City, UT 84109.

to relax, the children then try the card again and are amazed at the color changes! The square on the card will be blue if the children are relaxed. They are then told that they can relax themselves at any time and then use the card to check to see if they have succeeded. This gives the children more of a sense of control over their own behavior. The imagery exercises are also designed to enhance self-esteem, a variable we find to be crucial in the healthy resolution of grief.

Week 2

After a brief check on the use of their biofeedback cards, the group leaders begin to talk about "feelings of grief." The students receive a "feelings" handout that emphasizes key emotions and a discussion is encouraged that focuses upon their own personal feelings. Sometimes children are encouraged to use the blackboard to draw a feeling. The *expression* of feelings is emphasized. Feelings are validated and the children are then taught "healthy" ways to express themselves. For example, they are told that anger is a normal, healthy reaction to grief and that it is all right to feel this way. However, hitting your sister or getting into fights at school are not healthy ways to express anger. Suggestions are given on useful ways to release anger—through physical activity, such as running, one-on-one basketball, artwork or writing. The children are *not* encouraged to work through their anger in the group setting since although the group is supportive in nature, it is not the place to act out one's anger.

One successful technique to help illustrate the importance of expressing feelings is to have the children write their emotions down on smooth rocks and then stuff the rocks in a paper sack. Balloons are then tied to the sack and the children can see how "stuffing" feelings keeps them from feeling light and free again. After much discussion about healthy ways to release feelings, the children go outside and release the balloons. Symbolically speaking, this also has value in helping children grasp the idea of "letting go."

Artwork has been one successful exercise to help release the tension of grief as well as to give group leaders additional information on each child. Children are asked to "draw a picture of grief and what it feels like." This is also a time when children are most comfortable sharing with each other as they draw and color. Comments such as "were you scared when you saw your dad in the coffin?" are more likely to occur in these less threatening settings.

Because children know that they are usually punished when they are naughty, it is important to check with the children to determine if any feel a sense of responsibility for the death of their loved one. This is most effectively accomplished by telling a story about a child who *did* feel responsible and then checking with the group to see if they agree with this child's feeling of responsibility.

Week 3

At this time, children fill out a "Memory Book" about their loved one. This book, published by Holy Cross Hospital, includes information about the person who died (their favorite foods, things that made them laugh, etc.), a place to write a letter to the person who died, a place for drawing feelings, a page for photographs, an obituary and a funeral program.*

This book is helpful to the children in several ways; it is a structured way for children to talk about the person who died, and it is quite helpful to have on hand for future occasions when children panic because they cannot remember their loved one. It is also a personal way to express any unfinished business they may have. Writing a letter to the person who died is very therapeutic in helping children say what they still need to tell their lost loved one. Older children can complete the "Memory Book" on their own, in or out of the group. Younger children often tell the group leader what they wish to express and the leader writes down the information for them. The "Memory Book" has space for children to write down things they "didn't like" about the person who died. This is important since many children tend to "idealize" the deceased. It helps make their loved one more human and puts their grief in perspective.

The children are encouraged to share their books with other family members. (Their letters to the deceased can be removed from the book and sealed in an envelope if the child feels this is too personal to share.) The sharing of the "Memory Book" with families also helps adults to become aware of how much children feel and hurt. This, in turn, often provides more "permission to grieve" outside the grief support group.

Week 4

The last night of group is spent summarizing the entire grief group experience. A video of the book *The Fall of Freddie the Leaf* by Leo

---

*Additional information on the "Memory Book" is available from the Bereavement Program, Holy Cross Hospital, 1050 East South Temple, Salt Lake City, UT 84102.

Buscaglia is shown and a discussion of the film ensues, tackling any last-minute thoughts or feelings about grief before the group ends. The importance of saying good-bye to one another and dealing with yet another "ending" is emphasized. Treats are frequently shared at this time.

ADDITIONAL IDEAS AND SUGGESTIONS

We have found that the support experience is most successful when information is presented in concrete ways, utilizing a variety of auditory and visual techniques. Children have made "grief stones" by painting a sad face on one side of a smooth stone and a happy face on the other side. A discussion follows about being able to be both happy and sad when you are grieving. The children often carry their stones in their pockets and use them very much like "worry beads."

The use of visual imagery has proved to be an invaluable tool in assisting children with grief issues. We have used imagery to help children who did not attend the funeral say good-bye to a loved one. Children who were not permitted to see the body, because adults felt it would have been too painful an experience, will often have nightmarish images of what their loved one looked like, particularly when the death was violent. Imagery can help children create a new, peaceful image of their loved one and can diminish the effects of their fantasizing.

CONCLUSION

We are convinced that a grief support group experience not only offers children "permission to grieve," but also can be considered a form of "preventive medicine." When children are able to experience their pain in a loving, supportive, nonjudgmental atmosphere, they are less likely to carry unresolved grief issues with them into adolescence and adulthood. They are also more likely to offer their own children permission and support during any grief experiences they may have. We also value the importance of teaching stress management strategies to children who will be able to use these tools in future stressful situations, such as problems falling asleep, test anxiety, and other difficult events.

REFERENCES

Buscaglia, Leo. *The Fall of Freddie the Leaf.* Thorofare, NJ: Slack, 1984.
Murdock, Maureen. *Using Guided Imagery with Children for Learning, Creativity and Relaxation.* Boston: Shambhala, 1987.
Pappa, Michael. *Sweet Dreams for Little Ones.* Minneapolis: Winston Press, 1982.

9

Convergent Groups: An Approach to Grief Counseling for Families

Wendy Wainwright

In 1985, counseling staff at Hospice Victoria began to perceive a gap in their provision of bereavement programs. An increasing number of children were experiencing the death of a family member in the hospice program and it became apparent that they did not receive the kind of consistent support staff felt was needed.

There were several reasons for the existence of this gap: parents were reluctant to bring their children in for counseling; children resisted being "singled out"; children's needs at the time of death were often not recognized by families; and staff were simultaneously dealing with pressures of time and lack of experience in this area.

Staff felt the most effective way to support these children was through a group experience, and the Saturday Morning Children's Grief Support Group came into being. Based on information found in the available literature and influenced by our program philosophy about death and grief and the personal experiences of participating staff members, the goal of this program was to support children in their process of "healthy grieving."

Since 1985, Hospice Victoria has offered at least two children's groups each year. Initially open only to those children who were part of the hospice bereavement program, participants are now referred through other community sources and may be grieving either prior to or after a death. As a result, the range of the types of losses experienced has become much wider, and consequently the program approach and content have altered to accommodate this shift.

After offering several children's groups, we began to wonder about what happened to the children when the group ended. Did they continue to receive support for their grieving from family, peers and teachers? Were there further opportunities to practice the skills learned during our program? Did others understand "healthy grief" and acknowledge the importance of its expression?

We were intervening with these children for a total of 12 hours over 8 weeks and then returning them to virtually unchanged family settings. While some parents were already very aware and supportive of the necessity of their child's grief process, many did not have the understanding or emotional energy to reinforce the experience or the learning that had occurred in the group.

Our decision to offer a concurrent parents' grief support group was a result of our recognition that, while we could offer children an opportunity to understand, acknowledge and express their grief (in a peer group), we could never provide for their needs in an ongoing way, as their parents could at home. Where parents had refused counseling or a support group for themselves in the past, we found that most were willing to participate in a group that they were told focused on their children's grief and how they, as parents, could learn to help them. Once this group got started, we found that the parents quickly shifted the focus from the children exclusively to their own grief and accompanying needs. This meant that our goals for the parents' group had to be broader than those for the children's group; not only did we want to support and educate them as the parents of grieving children, but we also needed to support and educate them about their own grief.

The peer support that automatically occurs in a group has become a powerful component of this program: having a safe place to share fears, mistakes, vulnerabilities and successes seems to enable parents to return to their daily lives with more energy, more tolerance and more understanding of their own and their family's grieving process.

PROGRAM GOALS AND OBJECTIVES

Our first step in developing both programs was to establish exactly what we wanted to achieve and why and how we intended to go about it. While these goals and objectives have been refined somewhat over time, the underlying philosophy and concepts have remained the same. We believe that grief is the healthy response to loss; that people must experience the process of acknowledging, confronting and then moving on from each loss and that the natural way to do this is within the context of their community. This process is facilitated by receiving appropriate information and support, having opportunities for expression, and appreciation of personal strengths. While approaches may vary, this applies to both children and adults.

The Children's Grief Support Group

Goal: To assist children in the process of healthy grieving

Objectives:

1. To bring grieving children together in a supportive and consistent environment.
2. To offer appropriate age-related grief support to children.
3. To put children's current grief into the context of the larger picture of life and its many inevitable losses.
4. To identify high-risk children and those with possible unresolved or complicated grief and refer them appropriately.
5. To have fun!

The Parents' Support Group

Goal I: To support and educate parents in their own grieving process

Objectives:

1. To facilitate peer support within the group.
2. To offer staff support both within the group and on an individual basis.
3. To give parents information about their own grief process.
4. To put the loss and its grief process into the context of life and its many losses.

Goal II: To support and educate parents about their children's grief

Objectives:

1. To offer parents of grieving children both formal and informal support.
2. To give parents information about children and grief.
3. To help parents facilitate their children's grief process.

PROGRAM INFORMATION

The Participants

Participants include hospice and community family members who are grieving over a death, either before or after the event.

The children's group consists of up to 12 children, aged 5 to 12, who will benefit from a group experience. Those assessed as being inappropriate for the group are offered individual counseling. Those with overly complicated or unresolvable grief receive individual counseling, as well as being able to participate as a member of the group.

The parents' group may include significant adults other than the parent, such as grandparents and guardians. While we prefer that the parents attend the group, children are not penalized if they refuse or are unable to do so.

The groups meet on eight consecutive Saturday mornings from 10:00 to 11:30. Saturday morning permits both working parents and volunteer staff to attend, while leaving the remainder of the day free for other activities. The program is offered twice each year, starting in January and October. We avoid holiday times and long weekends as they tend to disrupt the group process.

The groups take place in separate rooms where the necessary facilities for each program are available. The children's group requires an open, warm, bright and washable space with access to the outside, as well as storage space for supplies and projects. The parents' group requires a comfortable and safe atmosphere. A private, "home-like" room, separated from the children's space works well.

The Staff

A facilitator and supplementary staff are required for each group. All hospice volunteers receive 30 hours of orientation, and those wishing to be involved with bereavement programs are required to do some additional training. Before starting with a children's or parents' group, staff receive a comprehensive package of information specifically related to working with grieving children, and they also must participate in an informal, one-day workshop.

The children's group is staffed by hospice volunteers and facilitated by university practicum students. The parents' group has always been co-facilitated by a practicum student as well as a counselor, primarily because we are still developing the program. It may also be that the information, authority and skill required by the adults exceed what we can expect from our students. Recent groups have also had a volunteer present, a welcome addition because he or she is a non-threatening support person.

The staff counselor has always been involved and responsible for the development, supervision and evaluation of both groups, as well as accepting and interviewing all children and parents referred to the programs.

Supplies

Supplies are dependent on the activities presented in each program. The children's group uses a lot of art supplies: paint, clay, fabrics, pastels, magazines and paper. They also receive a number of "gifts" during the program, such as fruit, drinks, "power rocks," photographs, "thunder eggs" and stickers. The parents' group requires a considerable amount of written material; for example, information about children and grief, weekly agendas, group activities and readings. They also receive a "gift" during the last session and usually require lots of coffee and refreshments during the sessions.

PROGRAM DESCRIPTION

The programs both stay the same and change every time they are offered. For example, we use the same basic format, address the same issues, and repeat certain content or activities in every group. However, the specifics always change according to the individual needs and particular losses experienced by the group members. Ongoing evaluation often suggests new ways of approaching issues and activities.

The sessions follow the same format each week: to give stability and ensure that there is a balance between discussion and activities. There is a clear beginning, middle and end to each session, as there is with the entire program. Each week has an underlying theme that reflects what we understand about death, dying, grief and the concerns of children and their parents. These determine the information shared, the activities presented and the gifts given to participants; each component is assessed in terms of age-appropriateness (for the children), of opportunity for learning, expression and sharing.

There are also a number of threads that run through all the sessions. For example, acknowledging and building on individual coping strengths, presenting grief as a healthy process, offering choices and alternatives, relating the current loss to life's other losses, and dispelling myths and misconceptions.

Weekly Format

All members of the children's and parents' groups meet in a common lounge prior to and after each session. This is a time for families and staff to meet together and become better acquainted. We also plan joint activities at this time.

THE CHILDREN'S GROUP

The children's group begins with the Opening Circle: members sit on the floor, talk about their week and decide on the words that would describe their "emotional temperature" that morning. Once the words are placed on the "thermometer," everyone returns to the circle and the session theme and activities are introduced. Information is presented in a variety of ways that may include telling stories, having question and answer time, puppets, games or discussions.

From there the group moves onto the session's Core Activity, which is intended to encourage further exploration of the information already obtained through expression of related feelings and thoughts, time for individual discussions and opportunities for additional learning. Activities could include painting, parachute games, working with clay, playing/listening to music, making personal shields, family maps or group murals.

Toward the end of the session, the participants gather for the Closing Circle. This can be a time to share projects with the larger group, to check for any gaps in information or misunderstandings that exist, to prepare the children for the week ahead and the upcoming session and to allow time to wind down before joining their parents.

Most sessions end with the sharing of food or giving of gifts that relate to the group learning or experience. These make the children feel really special and help hold their attention right up to the end.

THE PARENTS' GROUP

The parents' group also has a weekly format that is adhered to quite closely. There is less emphasis on activities and more time for discussion and group sharing than in the children's group.

The first task is for the parents to decide on their individual "temperatures" and place them on to the "thermometer." These are then used as a starting place for Check In, when each person has time to talk about the week. No discussion of children is allowed!

Next comes a short reading, thought or poem that relates to the session theme. This is followed by the work portion of the session which could be reviewing handouts about children and grief, completing personal worksheets, watching a film, dealing with particular issues by brainstorming or doing role plays.

The parents' group session usually closes with the presentation of some kind of "homework" for the parents (and/or their children) to try to do during the week, for example, giving appreciations, creating collages, reading prepared materials or related books, and thinking about some aspect of their life (rituals, messages received, or current stresses). Parents are given a summary of the theme, goals and activities presented during the children's session. They can use this information between sessions as a guide for talking to their children about grief. This is followed by a closing poem, proverb or story that seems to be appropriate in some way for the group and its members.

Weekly Themes

The program themes change very little from one group to the next. They are intended to reflect our goals and objectives for each program, indicating our understanding of and experience with the grieving of both children and adults, as well as their own concepts of death and dying, related concerns and myths.

Space does not permit a lengthy exploration of the themes we have developed in this chapter; however, the phrases or titles used in the sessions are given below:

Children's Group	*Parents' Group*
Getting acquainted	Getting acquainted
How does grief feel?	Childhood grief
Group cooperation and fun	Family rituals/ Interconnectedness
What happens when someone dies?	Our own grieving
Questions and answers about death and dying	Helping children grieve
Using our imaginations	Life and its stresses
Our family ties	My tree of life (Who am I?)
Saying good-bye	Saying good-bye

Weekly Activities

In the children's group, as mentioned, the activities are chosen to facilitate the learning that has hopefully occurred during the Opening Circle. The children always have a choice about whether or not they want to participate, but they seldom select to do something different. Usually, they work in small groups or individually with an adult; the one-to-one attention is particularly important for those unable to talk or ask questions in front of the larger group, although most the children seem to enjoy it.

Most of the activities can easily be adapted to the various age groups present; their interest certainly wanes when we forget or do not succeed in doing that. During projects geared toward the younger ages, the older children are often enlisted as helpers. At other times, the youngest group members may require individual attention to prevent them disrupting the group and its process.

In the parents' group the activities chosen tend to be cognitive in nature: for example, pen and paper exercises. We tried art projects with early groups and they were less than well received. That is not to say that they *won't* work, just that they *did not* work for us.

The parents in our groups really like the written handouts we have developed about grief and its manifestations, children's general responses and understanding of death and age-specific information. They also enjoy doing exercises related to the messages they received about grief during their own childhoods, their current life stresses, their roles and responsibilities and family rituals regarding death. In other words, while parents want information and help with their children's grief, they also need a lot of information and support for themselves and will take all they can get.

TYPICAL ACTIVITIES

Children's Group	*Parents' Group*
Making personal shields	Group information and sharing time
Feeling game and bags	Childhood losses or messages
Parachute games	Family rituals
Stories and working with clay	Phases of grief
Lots of painting and role-playing	Age-specific information
Visualization and music	Life stress rating chart
Family maps	Tree of life: roles and responsibilities
Group review: evaluation, murals, photographs	Group review: evaluation, preparation for future

THE FUTURE

The past has certainly been one of learning during an experience—very few of us have the opportunity to know ahead of time how to react to a sudden, or even expected death and how to help others—and that has been truly nerve-racking and challenging. We have had our fair share of disasters and triumphs: sessions where the entire group has refused to participate in some activity, fights erupting, screaming children who would not leave their parents, and staff who could not agree on the agenda, approach or activities. Some weeks only one or two group members have shown up. In our first group, we planned each session as we went and weren't even sure if it was all right to talk directly to children about death!

Through all of this, we have always managed to create a safe place, with adults who were, or became, comfortable with death and expressing their feelings and, at times, even displaying outrageous behavior. Most of all, despite inevitable problems, we have never stopped learning and growing as a program and as individuals, and we have never stopped having fun!

As a result of our experiences with children and in keeping with our philosophy that grief is everyone's concern, we have recently published a manual called *When Children Grieve*. It is intended for individuals and groups who wish to offer a support group like ours. Its easy-to-use format details the theory, practical considerations and layout of an eight-week program. Hopefully, a manual for offering a parents' group will follow.

The future will see these groups continue at Hospice Victoria, and more groups are likely to be established throughout the world as well. Recently, adolescent grief support groups started in one of our local schools, and they have been well received. Perhaps one day family support groups will also be offered, where parents and children have the opportunity to learn together and to help and support each other. It seems the only real restrictions for any of us are time and energy.

10

Alternative Approaches in the Treatment of the Bereaved Child

Corinne Masur, PsyD

The greater part of the literature related to childhood bereavement describes either theoretical formulations of the effect of loss on children, considerations of the effect of loss in childhood on the development of psychopathology in adulthood, individual case reports or—when intervention is addressed at all—intervention in the medical or school setting. Very little has been written specifically about outpatient psychotherapy with bereaved children. This chapter discusses, in general, a variety of strategies available to therapists or caregivers for approaching the evaluation and treatment of bereaved children; it presents three examples of cases treated; and discusses some of the questions and difficulties that arise in treating the bereaved child.

It has come to my attention, following years of treating children and reading the literature on complicated versus non-complicated grief reactions and pathological versus non-pathological reactions to loss, that there is no typical case of bereavement, especially when children are concerned. When a young parent dies, circumstances are always complicated, and as such, our responses as therapists must, by necessity, be sufficiently flexible to take into account the various needs of the grieving and often disorganized family. In order to address this, I will present three very different cases, each of which was treated by a different modality. The first case of a 6-year-old boy whose mother died of leukemia when he was 2. After her death he was placed in foster care. He is being seen in long-term individual therapy. The second is the case of a 10-year-old girl whose father was murdered by his girlfriend for whom he had left my patient's mother. She is being seen in short-term individual work. And the third is the case of a family, a mother and three boys, ages 9, 12, and 14; their father went out to play tennis one day and never came back, having suffered a heart attack on the court. They were seen in brief family therapy.

Before beginning with the cases, however, it is necessary to discuss briefly the evaluation of the bereaved child and the manner in which the clinician decides whether or not treatment is warranted. Rafael (1983) noted that children often present to practitioners following a bereavement with symptoms that may appear pathological, but are actually transitory reactions to the trauma of loss. According to Rafael, these children may be incorrectly enrolled in treatment. As Freud said in *Mourning and Melancholia*, in the case of adults, grief and mourning are expected reactions to loss and do not, in general, require therapeutic intervention.

Freud went on to discriminate between mourning and depression. Similarly, in child work, we must learn to separate grief and mourning from depression and significant indications of mourning gone awry from transient, reactive symptomatology (i.e., pathological behavior requiring treatment from non-pathological behavior). In order to decide upon whether therapy is appropriate, it is critical to determine the level of the child's difficulty engaging in the mourning process and adjusting to the loss, as well as the level of support available to the child. If therapy is deemed necessary, the type of treatment needed must then be determined. Often children are engaged in treatment simply because they are brought to the clinic by their families and they are automatically provided with the treatment assumed to be most suitable to their level of distress or psychopathology without determining whether or not treatment is even necessary in the first place.

The evaluation of the bereaved child's status in the grief process is an area that requires a great deal more attention than it has received so far. I find this problem of deciding whether or not the child requires intervention in their grief a thorny one. I will provide the guidelines that I personally use, gleaned from my experience as well as from recent studies and also how to perform this type of evaluation. In addition, I will offer recommendations for treatment of bereaved children.

PROCEDURE

To start, I take a detailed developmental history as well as a history of the child's experiences with loss, including the one for which he is presenting. I am concerned with pre-bereavement functioning, especially as it compares to the child's current functioning, the exact nature of the child's relationship with the person who died, specific details concerning what the child was told at the time of the death (if any), how death itself was explained (if at all) to the child prior to this loss, exactly what the child witnessed, whether the child attended the viewing or the funeral and what his reactions were, the presence or absence of various regressions, whether or not the child overtly displays sadness, the presence or absence of any behavioral problems, changes in school performance or peer activities, the child's response to recent separations, the child's questions about the loss, and the status of individual family members with regard to their own mourning processes.

In evaluating the material gleaned from this history taking and following one or more play sessions with the child, or family sessions (with the entire family), I make a decision regarding whether or not treatment is warranted. First and foremost, my perspective is developmental. I evaluate the child's reaction from the point of view of his or her age and stage of development.

For example, following the loss of a person important to him— a parent for instance—the child under age 5 is likely to experience regressions. He will also often have separation difficulties, sleep disturbances, eating disturbances, nightmares and confusion regarding the death. For children suffering a recent death—especially of a loved one—these reactions are expected. They may be transient. However, given the relative immaturity of a young child's ego and cognitive capacity, his great need for the presence of both parents and the stability of the family, and the likelihood of confusion regarding his own role in the death and his own mortality, I generally recommend treatment for all bereaved children of this age who have lost an immediate family member.

For children aged 5 and over, any prolonged symptomatology, especially depression or any marked absence of response to the loss, is an indication that evaluation is necessary. The children who are referred to a therapist years after a loss for a seemingly unrelated symptom generally fall into this category. The following is a list of specific factors that indicate the need for treatment.

1. The personality of the child prior to the loss was either very temperamental or very withdrawn (Elizur and Kaffman 1983).
2. The child had adjustment difficulties prior to the loss (Elizur and Kaffman 1983).
3. Suicide was the cause of parent or sibling death.

4. In the case of parental death, marital discord and/or divorce occurred prior to the death.
5. A very poor relationship with the lost relative existed prior to the death.
6. The remaining parent is unable to function "normally" after 6 months following the loss (Elizur and Kaffman 1983).
7. There is currently a very poor relationship between the child and the surviving parent.
8. The parent or sibling who died was mentally ill and resided with the family prior to death (Kliman 1968).
9. The remaining parent is very restrained in mourning and unable to share emotions and memories with the child (Elizur and Kaffman 1983).
10. The remaining parent is mentally ill.
11. The death occurred unexpectedly or abruptly.
12. The parent or sibling died following a prolonged or pain-filled terminal illness.
13. The parent died of cancer that involved the reproductive organs when the child was prepubertal or in adolescence.
14. The death was an unusually violent one (for example, if it was caused by another family member).

Strategies of Treatment

Whatever strategy is utilized, the purpose of treating a bereaved child is to help him allow his mourning to take place and to prevent any developmental interferences from occurring. The goal is to decrease feelings of denial, increase his ability to express his feelings, and help him to do the work of mourning—thereby facilitating the continuation of the normal, developmental process. Death is part of life, and in order to "keep on going" one *must* grieve; the process of grieving is a necessary part of living.

Parent Counseling

As Robert Furman wrote, "When a child's reaction to loss is basically adaptive, all efforts of the clinician should be directed toward a removal of any external threats." That is, when the child's reaction to loss occurs without any sign of pathology or developmental interference, clinical intervention should focus on insuring that the child's needs will be met throughout the period of mourning. In the case that the caretakers are unable to provide an environment that facilitates the child's mourning, parent (or caretaker) counseling is advisable.

The surviving parent, not unexpectedly, experiences extreme difficulty in adapting to the loss of the spouse. In a study of 14 bereaved families, Rafael (1977) found that all but one surviving parent experienced a pathological grief reaction. In such cases, the parent should be referred to psychotherapy. For example, Clark (1964) presents the case of a 25-year-old, previously well-functioning woman who sought treatment for her 2½-year-old daughter following the sudden death of her husband. The little girl had begun to suffer sleep disturbances and a general decrease in affective responsivity, especially with regard to her mother. Following an evaluation in which it was found that the mother felt overworked, cut off from adults her own age and unable to express her grief, a short-term treatment was initiated. When the mother was educated to the needs of her daughter and taught how to mourn the loss of her husband, her daughter's difficulties cleared. As well, the mother was more amenable to establishing new relationships.

For the parent who does not seem in need of psychotherapy or who is not open to such a suggestion, then parent counseling may be initiated. There are many critical issues to be worked on with the parents (if they are caretakers) of a bereaved child. Perhaps the first area of importance in working with the parent (grandparent, or surrogate parent) is to help them to understand that the child's experience of loss is not the same as theirs. The child neither experiences the specific loss nor understands death (that is, its place in life) in the same way as an adult does. The adult must therefore be educated to the limitations of the young child's ability to understand death cognitively at his particular developmental level. The parent must also be helped to understand the loss from the child's emotional perspective. For example, while most people view the death of a spouse as overwhelming, there is more of a chance that a parent can, with time, attain perspective and see that the pain from the loss need not last forever; in fact, an older person will probably realize that he can go on with life and perhaps even marry again. For a child, the loss of a parent, especially early in life, is a loss like no other. A child can never have another father or mother. In explaining his experience of loss, an adult whose mother died when he was 3 years old described it as feeling as though (in adult terms) his wife had died, all of his children had died, his house had burned down and he had lost all of his friends, as well as his means of communicating. He said that the loss of his mother at that age had sent him into a state of complete confusion and anxiety.

By aiding the bereaved child, the parent assumes an important role for himself during a time in which he might otherwise feel quite helpless. One of the first tasks the parent should be helped to do is to explain death to the child. Particularly during the time immediately following the loss, it is of great help for the child to feel that death is a subject that can be discussed. Depending on the child's developmental age, the explanations offered will differ. When addressing a very young child, the adult should stay on a very concrete level. It is necessary to explain that the all biological processes have stopped, that the deceased cannot breathe, eat, talk, walk or even come back. The method of burial or cremation is also an important issue to discuss. Moreover, it may be helpful to explain that if the parent could return he would do so, but that people who have died cannot "come back."

INDIVIDUAL TREATMENT

For children whose distress does not seem to improve with parent contact, children whose symptoms are particularly pronounced or children who have more than one of these factors, individual psychotherapy may be recommended. Such therapy is aimed at understanding the child's inner experience of the loss, removing obstacles to experiencing the affects associated with mourning, correcting conscious and unconscious misunderstandings regarding the loss, and modifying overidentification and overidealization of the lost loved one. Either long- or short-term treatment may be recommended.

FAMILY TREATMENT

In cases where the child's distress or symptomatology seems connected to a disorganized family situation, family treatment may be recommended.

Bereavement affects the family in many ways. As Rafael noted, the death of a family member means that the family system is irrevocably changed. Interlocking roles, relationships, interactions, communications, psychopathology and varying needs can no longer be fulfilled in the same way as before the death. The family unit as it existed dies along with the lost member, and a new family system must be built. The death is a crisis for the family unit as well as for each individual family member and each family subsystem.

Rafael also noted that children desperately need the stability of family life as they know it. Should the family become chaotic or disrupted, then their ultimate adjustment to the loss is in great jeopardy. On the other hand, if they are overly protected from experiencing the loss or if there is an avoidance or downplaying of their reactions by other family members, then their chances of recovery are also in jeopardy.

GROUP TREATMENT

Children's bereavement groups are also useful for homogeneous groups of bereaved children who are not in need of individual treatment. It is recommended that children whose parents were murdered or who suicided be included in groups specifically with other children having experienced the same type of loss. These kinds of bereavement groups can decrease the isolation and loneliness of children and enhance their ability to cope.

CASE EXAMPLES

The following case examples reveal the variety of questions that emerge in the course of evaluating and treating bereaved children.

The Cabbage Patch Kid

Jake is a 6-year-old Jewish/Protestant boy who currently resides in an upper-middle-class home with his 10-year-old brother, John, four foster siblings (all older) and his foster parents. When Jake was 1 year old, his mother, a drug addict, contracted leukemia. At 18 months, Jake (and John) went to live with their maternal aunt because of their mother's illness and because their parents had marital difficulties. When he was 2, Jake's mother died, and when he was 4½, his aunt, who was married and had one child of her own, decided that she could no longer care for the boys. Their father agreed to take them but continually put off the move until finally, after many missed visits and unkept promises, he disappeared altogether. Jake and John then went to live with a foster family, the Samuelses, on an emergency basis. The Samuelses, a well-organized, achieving family, had originally volunteered to accept one foster child, preferably a girl under the age of 4. Instead, they accepted two older boys.

When Jake first presented for treatment, he was an adorable, blond-haired, 6-year-old boy who was encopretic, accident prone and unable to perform in school. His foster mother was at her wit's end and demanded, appropriately, that the foster care agency fund psychotherapy. I evaluated him and recommended twice-weekly treatment. However, due to the foster family's schedule, he was started in once-weekly treatment.

On the second visit, Jake said to me, "I have a record that makes me cry every time I listen to it. You're a worry doctor and that's a worry, isn't it?" I asked him to bring the record with him the next time he came, and he did so.

It was a Cabbage Patch record and he played the entire thing for me. Finally, he indicated the song that he had previously referred to. He sang along with it and acted out all the events. The song concerned two Cabbage Patch Kids who had gotten lost from the cabbage patch and couldn't find their way home. It was night time, and they were very scared. They wandered and wandered and cried and cried until they finally found the cabbage patch. The record ended with all the Cabbage Patch Kids lying down to sleep and each one dreaming of the perfect family who might, one day, adopt them. During this song, Jake lay down on the floor, put his thumb in his mouth, and closed his eyes.

Later in the treatment Jake became very attached to a small stuffed monkey. Each time he would beg to take the monkey home. When I reminded him that it was best to leave the monkey in the office with me where he could play with him during each visit, he would tenderly put "Monkey" to bed. I was torn about this, realizing that Jake might need a transitional object to tide him over the long week between visits, but I felt that his taking the monkey home with him would probably end the availability of that material to me. Finally I compromised by allowing him to take little pieces of clay from the office each time.

Most recently, Jake's play has centered around his pretending to feed "Monkey" spinach and iced tea to make him strong. One day Jake got a little of the green clay on "Monkey's" face and couldn't get it off. As a result, "Monkey" supposedly pushed him in the trash can and continued to do so for many weeks.

Nancy

Nancy was a 10-year-old black girl from a middle-class home. On Halloween her father was killed by his girlfriend. Nancy's parents had been divorced for 5 years and her mother had remarried. She had a 4-year-old sister. Nancy's mother told me that just prior to her father's death, the family puppy had been run over by a passing car and that a year ago Nancy's grandfather had died.

Nancy presented due to acting-out behavior in school. While she had been well behaved previously, during the winter following her father's death, she had begun to call out in class and brought attention to herself in a number of other ways that disrupted the classroom.

When Nancy saw me for the evaluatory first visit, I asked her what kind of a doctor she thought I was. She replied, "You're the kind of doctor that helps kids stop having certain thoughts." When I asked her why she thought she was coming to see me, she said, "Because of my dad's death." When I suggested that perhaps she was having certain thoughts that she wanted to stop having about her dad, she readily agreed.

After meeting just three times and discussing her memories of her dad, her puppy and her grandfather, and her understanding of their deaths, Nancy's behavior in school had vastly improved. She was getting certificates each week for good behavior. Because Nancy wanted to continue with me, I recommended to her mother that we consider a short-term extension of the treatment, and Nancy continued to see me for 2 months, once weekly.

The Browns

Mrs. Brown called the clinic, complaining that each of her three boys had reacted differently to the sudden death of her husband, and she did not know if this was appropriate. In fact, she said that her 12- and 14-year-old sons had both cried openly, but her 9-year-old son had not. I saw the Brown family together. Mrs. Brown discussed her concerns regarding her 9 year old, and each boy made a few comments about his memories of his dad. I commented that all people have their own individual ways of grieving and moreover that at different ages, children demonstrate grief differently. Mrs. Brown seemed relieved, as did the boys, who appeared to be healthy, active, achieving children who did not want to spend time in a therapist's office. After two sessions, our contact ended with the exception that I recommended that Mrs. Brown might want to talk with someone about her own adjustment to her husband's death. She said, however, that she did not think this would be necessary.

Discussion

It is clear from these three cases that in each one bereavement was both unique and complicated. In the case of Jake, he had suffered multiple and sequential losses very early in life. Not only had he lost his mother to leukemia, but eventually he also lost his father due to abandonment and then his aunt in her role as surrogate mother.

Jake's material in treatment indicated his feelings of sadness, loneliness, and fear, as well as his yearning for a permanent replacement family. Depicting himself as a lost Cabbage Patch Kid was poignant indeed. The Cabbage Patch Kids have no real parents. Jake must also have felt parentless, and like the children on the record, he felt lost in a dark and scary world.

Moreover, in his play with "Monkey," Jake indicated his feelings of personal responsibility for having been abandoned. He must have done something bad (getting spinach on "Monkey's" face) in order to have been "thrown in the trash."

Additionally, Jake demonstrates many of the concerns typical of a 2 year old. He provides an example of the child who suffers a traumatic loss during this early period and who retains concerns from this stage of development well into later years. Jake's treatment, then, is aimed at correcting his mistaken feelings of responsibility for his rejection and abandonment, as well as at helping him express his feelings about his many losses. This was done through play therapy, the play being symbolic of his actual concerns.

Nancy's loss and her experience following it was at the same time both different and similar to Jake's. Nancy experienced the death of her father as a 10-year-old living in a stable home situation. While Nancy also experienced multiple losses (her grandfather, her puppy and her father), she had attained greater developmental maturity at the time of the loss and she lived in the more stable environment of her mother's and stepfather's home.

However, Nancy's loss was complicated by at least two factors. First, her father's death was a violent one, and second, within Nancy's immediate family, she alone mourned the loss of her father. Her mother did not report any sadness over her ex-husband's death. He had treated her badly during their marriage, in fact beginning to see the woman who ultimately murdered him while her mother was pregnant with Nancy.

Nancy's mother was not able to understand her daughter's upset, either cognitively or emotionally. Nancy's mother's insensitivity to Nancy's need for a place to express her sadness and her worries was demonstrated when, after three initial sessions and significant behavioral improvement on Nancy's part, her mother did not bring her back for subsequent sessions. When finally I requested that she bring Nancy in, it turned out that she told Nancy that I was "sick" because she felt that Nancy was better and did not need to come back. It was only after I explained that separation and sudden loss were exactly what had caused Nancy's symptoms and concerns in the first place that her mother saw the need to end her treatment more gradually—over a 2-month period.

The case of the Brown family was also different. This family appeared to be a well-functioning unit in which the death of the father caused the mother to have concern for the welfare of her boys. It was clear that roles had changed within the family, that the mother had attempted to take on both parental functions and that she was overwhelmed. However, once she felt that it was in fact "okay" for each child (and for herself) to mourn in their individual, age-appropriate ways, she did not wish further intervention. This case provides an example of the flexible family unit that can adapt to change and support one another, and that does not want the intrusion of "professional" help for any extended period during the time of their grieving.

CONCLUSION

It is clear that bereaved children require a spectrum of services to meet their individual needs. Complicated, traumatic, or very early loss resulting in pathological grief or, just as important, the absence of grief may require long-term individual treatment. Other types of loss and reactions to loss may be best approached by the host of other types of possible intervention, as described previously in this chapter. Both community mental health centers and private practitioners must be aware of and sensitive to each child's and family's needs, and educated as to the myriad possibilities for appropriate treatment.

REFERENCES

Elizur, E. and Kaffman, M. Factors influencing the security of childhood bereavement reactions. *Am. J. Orthopsychiatry* 53(4), 668–676, 1983.

Freud, S. *Mourning and Melancholia: Standard Edition*, Vol. 14. London: Hogarth Press, 1957.

Furman, R. A. Death and the young child: some preliminary considerations. *Psychoanal. Study Child* 19, 321–333, 1964.

Kliman, H. *Psychological Emergences of Childhood*. New York: Grune & Stratton, 1968.

Rafael, B. Preventative intervention with the recently bereaved. *Arch. Gen. Psychiatry 34*, 1450–1454, 1977.

———. *The Anatomy of Bereavement*. New York: Basic Books, 1983.

11

Children and Funerals

Brian McGarry

Ernie Coombs ("Mr. Dressup") of CBC television in Canada, wrote the following Foreword for an Ontario Funeral Service Association booklet entitled "Helping Children Understand Death," written by Vernon F. Gunckel, PhD.

Many years ago, my son Chris, then 4 years old, came up to me as I was talking on the telephone and tearfully put this question to me: "Why did he die so little?" It wasn't until I had finished my "important business" on the phone that I learned what Chris's question was about.

One of his newly acquired young guinea pigs had suddenly died. To a 4-year-old, a young animal should not die. As I tried to comfort Chris, I began to realize how inadequate my explanations were. This was his first direct experience with death—human or animal—and it was important that I give him good answers. Yet the more I tried to explain, it seemed that I raised more questions than I answered. Experienced as I was in educating and entertaining children through television, when it came to dealing with a tough subject like death face to face with my son, my ratings were pretty low.

I found myself wondering why this was such a difficult job. As an adult, I had experienced many situations involving death. Surely I could draw on my own previous reactions to find some sensible, satisfactory answers to my son's questions. Of course I could—but I realized that my reactions were *adult* reactions. What makes sense to an adult can seem like nonsense to a youngster.

It would be a more difficult situation if a friend or family member had died instead of my son's pet. Still, my experience showed me that discussing the subject of death—regardless of who died—with children is not a simple matter, and my previous experiences with death did not automatically prepare me for an event like this.

When the time comes for us to talk to our children about death, the methods chosen for use will vary considerably from child to child and certainly from one occasion to another. It is important to know what to say, how much to say, and the best time to broach the subject. Some of us may be fortunate enough to have the instinct to deal naturally with the situation. For most, however, guidance and information from an outside source is necessary.

Certainly if we ourselves are also grieving, it will ease our own stress if we are assured that we are communicating with our children in the best way.

Death is a difficult, distressing subject, but one we all must be concerned with. The purpose of this booklet is to inform and support you when the subject of death needs to be explained. If it eases the process for you, it will be sure to benefit your child.

This booklet recognized the role that funeral service personnel play in the grief process and the difficulty everyone has in explaining death to children. I will highlight a few areas covered by the booklet and then move on to my more personal experiences as a funeral director at Hulse & Playfair Homes in Ottawa.

Dr. Gunckel alerts us that among the early questions a child may ask about death are: What is dead? Why do people die? Where do dead people go? and What do dead people do? In the preschool years, a child's concept is centered on the idea that death and life are interchangeable—that they are reversible. Dead people can come back. This belief is often supported not only by the games they play, but also by television where a person can be killed in one program and found alive and well in another.

Dead people only go away for awhile—they take a trip—and then come back. Young children attribute life and consciousness to the dead. Dead people eat; they play; they do much that we do. Death can be avoided. Death is usually associated with accidents or getting killed through violence. If you are careful, you can keep from being dead.

Grown-ups can choose whether they live or die. To young children, parents are all-powerful. They can do just about anything. Therefore, being in command of all things, adults choose their coming and going. A parent's death may be viewed as rejection or punishment. A child may think that the reason his mother died was that he did something wrong or that he didn't love her anymore. A child may exhibit exemplary behavior, hoping that the dead parent will forgive him and return.

An element of magic also plays a major role in the world of the young child. Who has not heard, "I wish you were dead!"? When it actually happens, children may believe that they caused the death.

The death of a parent is associated with security, stability and dependability. "Who is going to take care of us now that Mommy is dead?" "Daddy, are you going to die?" These are common concerns for a child when a parent has died. The routine of everyday life has been interrupted, thus creating worries about the future. It is not unusual for a child to check the remaining parent's bedroom at night to see if the surviving parent is still there. There is frequently a fear that the other parent may also die.

Abstract concepts such as final, permanent, distance, and time cannot be understood in the same way that adults know them. For the young child, "now" is the most important moment—never mind tomorrow.

By the age of 5, a child's concept of death changes considerably. Death is no longer something that can be controlled. Death now comes from outside sources such as disease and growing older. This is the age of fantasy and monsters. New anxieties come to the fore. Ideas about the world greatly change.

With this understanding of a child's concept of death, we can become more sensitive and accepting of a child's feelings and actions. This understanding enables us to give comfort and support to children in their expressions about death.

A funeral director can relate very well to all of Dr. Gunckel's statements, and we can add a few more questions to his list, questions that come forward in the funeral home setting:

- Where are grandpa's legs?
- Does grandpa have socks on?
- Can we touch him?
- How do you embalm?
- What do you do (as a funeral director)?
- Why are there flowers?
- What happens with cremation?
- Can I see the inside of the hearse?

We don't pretend to be grief psychologists, but our daily experience does provide empirical information that can be helpful to those concerned with the necessity of relating appropriately to children at the time of a death.

The funeral company of which I am a part conducts between 1,300 and 1,400 funerals per year. Most of the funerals include some children's involvement, although there are services where children are conspicuous by their absence.

One of our greatest faults as adults is that we sometimes forget that children are people, too. They react to traumatic situations with such emotional overtones as disbelief, bodily stress, anger, guilt, anxiety and panic—just as adults may do. Children often act out their feelings in ways that do not seem appropriate to an adult. But children may not be able to say what they feel with words, so they must depend on body language and behavior to vent their feelings. Adults should be perceptive and understanding of what this behavior really means. Even so-called delinquent conduct may well be an acting out of grief, an expression of the child's insecurity.

A child growing up today is more aware of death than most parents realize; yet it is a subject that adults usually avoid. Such a repression of reality only magnifies the youngster's fears and replaces truth with fantasy and psychological defenses. Therefore, when a loved one dies, children should be allowed to express their grief. If they are deprived of the natural emotion of grief, the consequences could prove harmful. Proper mental health for children and adults alike depends on the acknowledgment of tragedy, not its denial. It is better to say to a child, "I would cry too," rather than "You must not cry."

Parents, then, are not doing their children a kindness by excusing them from attending a funeral. It is a mistake to send the child away with a friend or relative until after the funeral. Instead, a child should be allowed to share in the service honoring the life of someone close. Many child psychologists agree that it is good to permit a child to attend a funeral; in fact, from about the age of 7, a child should be encouraged to attend, provided the child is not strongly opposed. In no way should one force a youngster who displays apparent fear. But attendance at even an earlier age may be permissible if the child has gone to church services or has been to other public gatherings.

A child is an integral part of the family unit and should be included on every significant occasion. Though sad, the funeral is a sharing community process and a crucial event in the life of every family. Being excluded leaves children with few facts and a lot of imaginings that may confuse their thinking. If a child is going to a visitation or funeral service, explain some of the details in advance. Tell him what to expect if he is going to view the body. Put him at ease by describing what will happen so he can better understand why it is being done. It is sometimes wise for the child's first visitation to be with only a few persons especially close to him. This will permit the child to react more freely and to verbalize feelings and concerns.

The conduct of adults, especially parents, during the period of the funeral can be helpful or harmful to a child in attendance.

Parents who express openly any feelings that move them, and who explain their emotions can do much to free the child to express his sense of loss at his own level. Do not protect the child unduly.

Of course the dead are to be remembered with appreciation, but after a short time the major energies of the bereaved must turn to those who live on. The child will want to talk, and not just be talked to. He should be given every opportunity to discuss his memories, but at the same time, he should be guided into talking about the future and how the family will adapt. Whatever we do, we must be careful not to attach adult-oriented meanings to the ways in which a child expresses his understanding of death. Never should we shame or criticize the responses he is making, but he should be aided in getting out of himself and into social activities appropriate to his age. The necessity for carrying on daily routines will assist the process of adjustment and, in time, special interests and pleasures will again assume their normal place in the scheme of things, both for parent and child.

Finally, adults must take care not to work out their own grief experience through the child. It is damaging to try to make the child an emotional replacement for the deceased. We must respect the child's own personality.

In the end, of course, what we are will determine what we teach our children. We communicate our feelings both consciously and unconsciously. The real challenge, then, is not just how to explain death to children, but how to understand and accept it ourselves.

An area of adult acceptance and understanding that is most important concerns our elementary and high schools. In one 1987 study, 98 percent of teachers felt it was important to deal with the topic of death in class as it arose, but 58 percent did not feel they were prepared well enough to do so.

In the book *Losing Someone You Love—When a Brother or Sister Dies*, young people expressed a desperate need to be heard. They looked for understanding but didn't usually find it in the family or school setting. Fran Newman, a guidance counselor with the Northumberland-Newcastle School Board, makes some valuable observations:

> I think we are all aware that we hide death in our society. Has anyone often or ever done a unit on death and dying? I was surprised to discover that 80 years ago, 65 percent of children under 15 died, while today only 3 percent do. Formerly death was much more present and made more visible. It happened at home and whole rural areas mourned together. Today 90 percent of people die in hospital.

Given that our students may not receive comfort, assurances or information from distraught relatives at home, and given that death is almost a taboo subject in some families, what is our [school] responsibility? Is it a should or a must? I think the answer to that lies in our compassion for these hurting children. For teachers with warm hearts, it is definitely a must.

The following are some suggestions for teachers and others facing similar circumstances. The suggestions are by no means exhaustive; one must assess each situation and each setting:

- Picture books can be helpful to children in the lower grades (progressive funeral homes have book lists which should be helpful and indeed have many of the books in their libraries).
- Sit on the floor with the children or on chairs at their level. Do not talk down to them; the young people will be much more open in a circle rather than in a scattered or more formal desk setting.
- Be truthful with the children; if a peer has died, it is best to address the fact of the death at the earliest opportunity. Provide accurate information and do not use euphemisms. However, as Fran Newman suggests from her experience as a teacher, "Be very aware of the double danger of saying too little or too much." The latter is particularly so if the death has been a suicide. Vernon Gunckel notes: "While not telling the child the truth can create difficulties later in life, it must be said that being too explicit can also present fears and misunderstanding. A child needs to know the truth, but only within his or her ability to comprehend and tolerate such expression."
- A teacher in the intermediate grades can expect a lot of weeping and it is helpful to have another resource person in the room.
- Allow time for questions and be understanding of different points of view resulting from different religious or family beliefs. In all instances the main concern is to support the bereaved child and his family and of course not to impose one's personal views.
- The teacher should watch for body language, particularly in the lower grades. As suggested earlier, sometimes feelings are not expressed verbally and may be expressed through play.

- No two children will grieve in the same way. Don't compare children. Children grieve intermittently and may ask to go out and play as though nothing has happened.
- Watch for withdrawal, a sudden drop in grades, or mood swings.
- Be a good listener.
- Some families find it helpful to make a scrapbook about the person who has died and to share memories in this fashion.
- Be prepared to make referrals when necessary.
- Be aware of relevant self-help groups in the area.
- Be knowledgeable about the value of the funeral and prepare the class if they are attending the service.

Fran Newman understands the role of the teacher and bereavement in the classroom very well when she states:

> It would be nice if you [the teacher] never had to deal with death as a part of our school curriculum or even as part of our lives. But we don't live myths and we don't live fairy tales. It needs all of our skill and all our love sometimes to be the best teacher we are capable of being. But it is worth the effort.

Dealing with the funeral of a child is the most difficult task a funeral director can confront, much more difficult than the death of an adult who has lived a fuller life. Not only is it difficult for the funeral director, but also for caregivers who may have been associated with the child (doctors, nurses, ambulance personnel, teachers, clergy). Add to this the normally severe grief experienced by the parents and siblings and one can begin to understand the trauma surrounding a child's death.

Humber College funeral service educators have offered on occasion a course designed to "help the helpers." Certainly by helping the helpers, caregivers are taking the first step toward being better professionals when confronted with similar circumstances surrounding a child's death in the future. One must understand the process of grief and children's death before being able to help others, particularly other children. One never becomes hardened to the grief process, but one can gain knowledge which in turn can help others. The importance of actualizing that the death has occurred and the significance of viewing the human remains; the need for support from others; the need to express sorrow—all of these needs can be appreciated. What appears foolish intellectually can be understood as emotionally necessary.

If there is any one fact I have grown to know in funeral service, it is that the intellectual acknowledgment of a death is quite different from its emotional acceptance; the latter must be attained for healthy recovery. Therefore, if a child or an adult makes a request such as the placement of a letter, a picture or a toy in the casket before burial or cremation, one should appreciate that the benefit is not for the deceased, but for the surviving sibling, spouse or friend. Funerals are for the living, and this truth is even more pronounced when it comes to the death of a child. The breakup of a marriage and guilt feelings on the part of a sibling are two common occurrences when a young person dies in a family, and as with an adult death, many family problems can be avoided if the right people are present or available.

Among the most important people to have available are those who have experienced the situation firsthand in their own families. Bereaved Families of Ontario is one example of an excellent self-help group that is readily available to assist parents and often siblings, too. No matter how professional bereavement caregivers have or will become, let us not overlook the obvious: the real experts are those who have come through tragedy and are able, eventually, to carry on productive lives.

Some final thoughts from Dr. Gunckel and the Ontario Funeral Service Association booklet seem appropriate:

> No matter how hard we may try, we cannot protect a child from an awareness of death. When riding in a car, we may pass a cemetery which prompts a question or two. The evening news, television, drama and film often portray death. Children themselves are sometimes caught up in 'death games' . . . When children ask questions about death, we may experience a sinking feeling and do everything possible to change the subject or gloss it over. In part, our first reaction may come from a general sense of personal inadequacy in being unable to answer any of the questions ourselves. As one person put it . . . before I can teach my children about death, someone has to set me straight.

Working together, funeral directors, educators, medical personnel, clergy and self-help groups can bring a new understanding to bereaved children and in so doing help assuage the sorrow of death.

IV

The Bereaved Family

12

When You Lose a Child, are You Still a Parent? When You Lose a Parent, are You Still a Child?

Sandra Kesselman Hardy, MSW, CSW

When it is a beloved who has died, besides the horror at the extinction of life, there is a severance, a spiritual wound, which like a physical wound is sometimes fatal and sometimes heals.
—Tolstoy

Nobody gets out of here alive, as the saying goes. Whoever we are, whether we are famous or unknown, surrounded by wealth or poverty, the end is the same for all of us. We are all simply guests in this world; all of us will, at one point, die.

The information presented in this chapter has largely been gathered from individual and group discussions with surviving children and from published literature. The information is divided into two sections: the first is based on individual support services provided by the Palliative Care team at the Ottawa Civic Hospital and by the Ottawa-Carleton Branch of Bereaved Families of Ontario (BFO); the second describes programs recently initiated by BFO to assist children in specific age categories in a self-help group setting.

THE CHILD

Our focus here will be on the emotional and social impact of a parent's death on children in the three age categories studied to date: 8 to 11 years, 16 to 30 years and over 30 years. Studies specifically related to pre-adolescents (12 to 15 years) have not yet been carried out.

Before we begin, you may be wondering why those over 30 are referred to as "children"? Obviously, once you are born and become someone's child, that relationship is fixed; everyone will always be a child in this sense. The child can be defined as the spontaneous, vulnerable, emotional part of ourselves—that part which comes naturally. Transactional analysis suggests that each of us exhibits three ego states: the parent, the adult and the child. In our studies, we found it is the childlike part of us that we get in touch with when we grieve.

A child can be described as a descendant in the first degree— an infant, a young person, a son or a daughter. We often consider childhood to be a magical time of life. It is not, however, an enchanted world where all longings are satisfied. It is only in the minds of adults that childhood is seen as a paradise and that children are innocent, protected and joyful.

One important difference between a child and an adult is that a child takes everything as a challenge, whereas an adult usually considers everything to be a blessing or a curse. Unencumbered by preconceptions, a child has the "wisdom" to approach each event as it is, not knowing its outcome, nor forcing results.

Psychologically, the basic concepts and essence of a child can be retained in adulthood, despite the chronological passage of time. While children symbolize life, growth and the future, death represents the complete opposite. Combining these extremes seems unnatural; but that is exactly what was found to occur in the three children's groups.

8 to 11 Year Olds

Erik Erickson, author of *Childhood and Society,* describes the task of 8- to 11-year-old children as one of learning the pleasure of working steadily and achieving goals. Unfortunately, grieving children suffer from poor concentration and an inability to persevere in tasks. Failure to achieve tasks successfully can lead to feelings of inadequacy or inferiority. This can reinforce their feeling different from the norm. Chris, a 10 year old, describes this well:

> After my dad died, I couldn't study, I couldn't remember anything at school. I felt so different.

This age group is concerned with the impact of death on themselves and on the interrelationships in their lives. The child's perspective about death is rapidly evolving and death is seen as movement and transition, though irreversible. In the words of Michael, an 11 year old:

Death is when you move to another planet or world.

Another 10 year old observed that

Death is when God says its time to come.

A third youngster described death quite unusually:

When you die, it's like a clock. It stops ticking and you don't move.

A frequent and understandable concept of death is the transference of the deceased to "another place." One method of transportation to the other place is via "Heaven Airways," as shown in a picture drawn by Matt, an 11 year old. In Matt's picture, even the pilot is not sure whether to smile or frown. Perhaps his feelings are confused as well.

Along with confusion, children invariably express feelings of sadness, fright, loneliness, disbelief, jealousy, anger, hurt or shock. The following quotations and observations illustrate some of these.

On loneliness:

Sometimes I talk with my friends if they bring it up first.

This child wanted support, but had trouble bringing up the subject.

On the protection of a surviving parent:

I don't want my mother to start crying, because if she cries a lot I worry she'll get sick and go to hospital. She has asthma. Then she's gone, too.

This child was unable to talk with his mother for fear of upsetting her and losing her.

On fear:

I think one of the rules of the group should be no laughing at anyone's feelings—ever.

It is important to record that in the 8- to 11-year-old counseling sessions, all but one of the group members were uncertain as to why they were attending. Each child had lost a father 6 months to 2 years prior to the group experience. Despite the length of time, the mothers had difficulty explaining the purpose of the group to their children. This seemed to be a reaction to their own grief. It was therefore necessary to clarify and elaborate the process in order to reduce the children's confusion.

As might be expected, the father's death had caused stress on the family unit—difficulties in the relationship with the surviving parent, sibling rivalry and problems in role identification. As an example, one 10-year-old Iranian boy felt that he had to model his father's behavior in order to remain close to him. In his words, "I began to lift weights like Dad did." His brother set up behavioral expectations both for his mother and himself, commenting, "She can have friends, but I'd kill her if she ever remarried. I don't need a new dad. I can help Mom."

These issues can and should be addressed in group counseling. In the final analysis, however, a mother's management of the situation will probably be the most important factor in its eventual resolution.

16 to 30 Year Olds

Similar emotions are mirrored in the young adult group—16 to 30 years of age. The boundaries in this age group are more nebulous because there are many variations in the young person's psychosocial development. The feelings are reflected in socially acceptable and personally rewarding behavior.

If feelings stem from hurt and anger, then behavior may be hostile, destructive and injurious to self-esteem. The stress of a death may propel a young adult to behave in a manner unrelated to the event or, on the other hand, to overcompensate and act out. During this age, it is normal for a young person to focus on body image. This may be confusing because bodies react to the physical manifestations of grieving—aches and pains, weight change or sleep disturbances. Such changes, thought temporary, may not be recognized as grief reactions and could well affect the developing self-image.

Often, surviving children in the young adult group will not feel normal and will express this by saying such things as:

I don't fit anywhere; I feel different.

> I felt embarrassed, unsure of myself, angry.

> I didn't feel my grief was anybody's business but mine.

They may emotionally withdraw from friends and family and try to isolate themselves.

The normal course of young adulthood is stormy but, with the additional stress of grieving, normal development and resolution may be hindered. One young woman caught in this struggle described it by saying:

> If I didn't love my mom so much, I wouldn't hurt so much. I'm afraid to get close to anyone.

Typically, the youth will feel isolated, as demonstrated by the following:

> No one else I know had a father that died.

> One thing that helps me is writing in my diary. It's really neat because it's like a friend who will listen to you.

Normally, young adulthood is a time spent consolidating a sense of identity—moving away from parents and exploring new people and places. Grieving, however, can dramatically impact this process:

> I feel like I'm lost—my roots that made me solid in front of obstacles are gone. Sometimes I feel like I'm wandering round looking for someone.

Young adults do not relate death to movement and transition in the same manner as 8 to 11 year olds. Instead, it is seen as an abnormal event that is imposed upon them.

> Death leaves you feeling helpless and rejected. There's nothing you can do. You could kill your loved one for leaving you, and yet you know it wasn't his fault.

> I hate them for dying. They couldn't help it, but I hate them.

It is normal to have these conflicting, crazy feelings about one's loss. The 16- to 30-year-old age group recognizes that death is irreversible and sees the concept as universal. Nevertheless, they feel distant from it personally.

After a death, young adults may avoid close, personal relationships because "it's just not worth it—the pain is too great." Quite often, however, they are eager to join a peer group, sensing perhaps that the group can replace their family. Sometimes there may be jealousy between siblings and conflict between family members that would not exist in a group. One 18-year-old, eldest sibling said:

> In a way it's hard to be the oldest because when you're small, like my sister, parents are more likely to take you into their arms and hug you. I'm too big to be picked up, but if I'm crying Mom will hug me and try to make me feel better. I want a little hugging without having to cry.

A 17-year-old girl spoke of the tension in her family when her mother remarried a year after her father's death from cancer:

> She wants me to call my stepfather Dad. I won't do it. She wants me to buy him a card on Father's Day. No way!

While this young adult may be expressing her own autonomy, the mother seems to be compounding the daughter's grief by asking her to accept a new dad too early in the grieving process.

Adults Over 30

The third group (adults over 30) tends to view death in terms of how the loss changes their identity—"I am an orphan." They see the parent-child relationship as unique, even if that relationship doesn't exist any longer:

> You can remarry, but you can only ever have one mother and father.

> No one can ever love me the way my father did.

Just as children and young adults are concerned about where the deceased goes after death, the adult is also concerned about the literal location: "Where is my spirit?" "Where is heaven?" These questions reflect the adult's personal and spiritual philosophy. Woody Allen, the comic philosopher, expresses his own anxiety about the afterlife. He sees heaven as a cocktail party, but fears no one will know where it is!

The adults in our program describe death as leaving them brokenhearted, destitute and cheated. In the words of one:

> Death is like a burglar who comes in the middle of the night and steals your most precious possession. When death leaves, you look

around at the mess—the destruction, the loss. You're furious, you've been robbed.

Many of the other feelings expressed by the adults are akin to those shared by children and young adults.

The main task of adulthood—to establish and guide the next generation—is inhibited by grieving, which is often a self-absorbing process. Grieving requires tremendous energy, which results in less energy for family and child-centered activities.

The experience of losing a second parent is different from losing the first. In some ways it may be made easier by knowing what to expect and how to respond. In other ways it may be much harder since it rekindles feelings of the first loss. There is no longer any sense of protection from death; you are the next generation. Though mature, your sense of loss may feel more like that of a child.

After losing a parent, the adult may feel trapped between caring for his own children and caring for the surviving parent. Often, feeling an added responsibility, the adult anticipates what life will be like when the second parent dies. These anticipatory feelings bring further guilt and resentment and must be dealt with to avoid later complications.

It may be thought easier to accept the death of an older parent. This, however, is often not the case. In the words of one woman whose mother died at age 90:

> I hate it when people say that she lived a full life. It's as if somehow I shouldn't feel sad she's dead. Because she's my mom, I'm her daughter and I'm feeling very sad. I'm going to miss her.

Sometimes the loss of a parent in adult life can act as a developmental spur, pushing sons and daughters into becoming full grownups. It imposes a new maturity on those who could not achieve it as long as they remained someone else's child. The loss evolves into a gain. We would be willing to forgo this gain to forgo the loss, but life does not offer this option. Adaptation is the only healthy choice. Accepting the difficult changes that loss brings can enable mourning to come to an end. As one adult woman confided:

> I will always have a mother, no matter what. I still have her memory.

Interviewing children of various ages has provided information about how the child in each of us grieves. Ironically, in the children and young adults interviewed, the children related as expected with spontaneity and excitement—emotions characteristic of childhood. The young adults, however, were more concerned with achieving adult status and did not perceive a child within:

> The death made me more mature and grow up quicker.

The adults, however, felt they were able to retain the child within themselves, in spite of their loss.

> I am better at being a child now at 40 than I was at 21.

> I still like to feel the child in me—the wonder and beauty of life.

> It is easier to express the child in me as an adult because I'm more comfortable with myself. I'm not trying to impress people.

DISCUSSION

It is traumatic for a child of any age to lose his parent. John Bowlby and others state that, to foster the best adaptation, children need:

1. A good relationship with the family before the death.
2. A reliable, comfortable caretaker after the death.
3. Prompt and accurate information following the death.
4. Encouragement to join in the family grieving.

These conditions can surely make a difference, but we must not forget that children live both within themselves and in the outside world. Each of the three groups we have studied face the emotional challenge of coping with overwhelming feelings of vulnerability and abandonment. It is this challenge that the child within each of us strives to meet.

The three group programs which have generated the study data, and of which we have spoken today, have offered survivors the opportunity to process their grief and to live their lives without their beloved parent.

The children's group consisted of five 8 to 11 year olds who met for six consecutive weeks. The group was led by two professionals and supported by an adult volunteer. Parental permission and information were obtained through a consent form and questionnaire. Parents were encouraged to participate through informal contact with facilitators. The therapeutic approach we utilized included drawings, story books, photographs and diaries. The goal of the approach was to promote sharing to elicit and normalize feelings in a non-threatening environment. This reduced the children's stress and their sense of isolation.

The young adult group was conducted over twelve sessions and offered support to ten participants in the 16- to 30-year age bracket. The group was co-led by two volunteers in the same age range. Each meeting began with a sharing of the events of the previous 2 weeks and discussion of specific reactions to grief—mental, emotional, physical, social and psychological. Utilizing photographs, journals, music and literature, the group members shared their experiences and feelings. An appreciation of joy and humor played an important role.

There were nine members in the parent-sibling or "over-30" group who met for twelve sessions. The group was co-led by two volunteers who had each lost a parent. For these people each loss had two facets—the loss of the parent in adult life and the childhood parent who loved and protected them. This group spoke about the intensity of the relationship and how, in spite of death, the relationship lived on. The facilitators utilized the concept of personal diaries or journals, books about parental loss, photographs and the sharing of common practical concerns such as wills and finances. Such an approach was found to be extremely beneficial in the emotional processing of grief.

Common to all three groups was an acute interest in where the deceased had gone and life after death. All groups were afraid they would forget their parents. In her unwillingness to let go, one young girl stated:

> I love sitting in Dad's chair, but I want to sit alone, because I don't want to share his memory with anyone.

The 8 to 11 year olds were the most prolific in terms of feedback of the group experience. They provided many comments and suggestions about what had helped. We concluded that the group experience should be longer, perhaps eight to ten sessions, but that the approach was very useful. A 9-year-old girl summed it up beautifully, saying:

> If I knew anyone whose father died, I'd invite her over a lot. It helps to have friends treat you like a normal person.

The members of the young adult and adult groups individually completed an evaluation referring to the group process, the facilitator leaders and the effect of their experience. By utilizing feedback from the participants it is hoped that future programs can be tailored to the needs and desires of those involved.

For all of our "children" and for the child in each of us, death arouses the need for connectedness and the continuation of relationships.

> We shared the lives we lived, shared delight, uncertainty, pain and frustration. We shared what we had the sense to share—it was a lot and it was good.

REFERENCES

Bowlby, John. *Loss*. New York: Basic Books, 1980.
Donnelly, K.F. *Recovering from the Loss of a Parent*. New York: Dodd, Mead, 1987.
Erickson, Erik. *Childhood and Society*. New York: W.W. Norton, 1963.
Gordon, Sol. *When Living Hurts*. New York: Union of American Hebrew Congregations, 1986.
Grollman, Earl. *Talking About Death: A Dialogue Between Parent and Child*. Boston: Beacon Press, 1970.
Myers, E. *When Parents Die: A Guide for Adults*. Toronto: Penguin Books, 1987.
Prichard, Elizabeth, et al. *Social Work with the Dying Patient and the Family*. New York: Columbia University Press, 1977.
Schiff, H.S. *Living Through Mourning*. Toronto: Penguin Books, 1987.
Viorst, Judith. *Necessary Losses*. New York: Random House, 1986.

13

Pastoral Care When a Child Dies

Beatrice M. A. Ash, MDiv

This chapter, written in case history format, concerns the death of children of all ages and at various stages of life development from 3 months gestation to 60 years of age and older. The parents discussed vary in terms of their marital status, age, their mental stability and their commitment to organized religion. The "children" discussed range in age from 3 months gestation to the early sixties, and the parents from 19 to the early nineties. I have a personal knowledge of each case history and in most cases have ministered to the parents or siblings with varying degrees of involvement. In each case the outcome of palliative care and bereavement management has been compared to a perceived desired response.

In order to protect the identity of the persons involved, all parents and children are referred to by names other than their own. Any other information that could lead to the identification of the subjects has been altered without losing the basics of the case. I have two main objectives in mind: to show that all parents suffer greatly from the death of a child and that sound pastoral care or secular support facilitates a more favorable outcome to the grieving process.

CASE 1: WILLFUL ABORTION

The first case concerns Mary, a 36-year-old woman from a small town. She had been married for 12 years before her marriage—which was childless—ended in divorce. Mary subsequently became sexually involved with her employer and, as a result, became pregnant. She did not consider any alternative other than abortion and her employer made an appointment for her to have an abortion at an outpatient clinic in a well-known hospital. Three days later, Mary went to the appointed room at a hospital. There were about 15 other women present, and a nurse was taking personal information from each of them. Mary was asked to wait and in turn she was taken to a small operating room. She was anesthetized locally and the abortion was performed. Three hours later Mary was sent home. By asking a doctor, an operating room nurse and two other women who had abortions several discreet questions, I found that Mary's experience was not uncommon.

Currently, Mary is seeing a psychiatrist in an attempt to learn to handle the guilt she feels and feelings of grief. Had she carried her child to term it would now be about 2 years old and every 2 year old that Mary sees becomes a projection of her aborted child.

CASE 2: ABORTION

Sarah knelt in the rear pew of St. Paul's Church, weeping. She had been in church for the past 2 hours praying for guidance, but she still had no clear direction as to whether she should end her 3-month pregnancy. Sarah was 38 years old, had been married to Peter for 15 years and had two daughters, 13 and 11, and a son, 9. Due to ill health, Peter had recently sold a reasonably prosperous retail business and was in the process of establishing a small manufacturing plant; he counted heavily on Sarah's money-making ability to help him in this venture. It would be very difficult for Sarah to work if she carried the pregnancy to full term.

Sarah had not been feeling well for some time, and 6 weeks earlier she had gone to see her family doctor. His diagnosis was that Sarah was beginning menopause, and because of her young age, he suggested that Sarah see a gynecologist to confirm his diagnosis. When she went to the gynecologist, he had done a pap smear and a pregnancy test. Both tests had been positive. The doctor recommended an immediate hysterectomy, which would, of course, end the pregnancy. He also had informed her that the malignancy was in a very early stage, that there was no possibility that it would harm the unborn child and that a 6-month delay in surgery would probably not mean that the disease would spread to other organs of the body. Sarah asked for time to make a decision and was informed that if an abortion was to be performed, it would be within the next 2 weeks. The doctor needed 10 days for planning and scheduling, so that only left 3 or 4 days for Sarah to make her decision.

Sarah had strong faith and was very active in her church. She had definite views on what was right and wrong, and she based these feelings on scriptural teachings and had been involved, nominally and financially, in the pro-life movement. When Sarah and Peter's oldest daughter had been 6 months old, Sarah discovered she was pregnant. Peter insisted that she have an abortion, and Sarah had done so. Since that time, Sarah had carried the guilt of her action. Peter's insistence on the abortion at that time had caused a rift that had only grown wider as the years passed.

Peter became a heavy drinker and occasionally was physically abusive. Over the years he even had affairs with other women. Sarah had been on the verge of leaving him several times, and 3 months ago had been to see a lawyer to gain information on her legal rights if she separated from him. Soon after Sarah had seen the lawyers, Peter broke off his relationship with his latest woman friend and promised to turn over a new leaf. It was soon after that Sarah had become pregnant. Sarah wanted to believe that he meant what he said, but she had been through this before and was, understandably, pessimistic.

Sarah had a few close friends, but they were also Peter's friends, so she felt that she could not turn to them for personal help. She had tried to discuss her family situation with her parish priest, but he refused to counsel her because it was a "personal" matter and he "didn't want to become involved". Sarah's family lived a thousand miles away, and a telephone call was an unsatisfactory way of discussing such a delicate matter. Sarah felt that God was her only source of help; however, at the present time she was so hurt and confused that she could not hear what He was saying.

The following are the issues that could, perhaps, have been pointed out by a pastoral counselor:

Children: The possibility of depriving the existing children of their mother and leaving them with an unpredictable father. Fairness to a new child in bringing it into the world to be nurtured by an older couple or, worse still, by an older single parent and with much older siblings.

Mother: Guilt feelings not resolved from years before, and another tie to an unstable marriage.

Father: In not consulting Peter on the subject, was Sarah writing off the marriage?

The reason for including the above case is to emphasize that even when all the criteria for an "approved" abortion seem to be present, it does not necessarily mean that it must be carried out. Sarah decided to carry the pregnancy through to term. However, due to complications, the child, a baby girl, was born 3 months early and weighed only 2 pounds; despite this, the child flourished from the beginning. A hysterectomy was performed soon after the delivery of the child, and no further malignant cells have been detected as of this writing, 15 years after.

CASE 3: STILL BIRTH

Anne and David were in their late twenties when they got married. For several years Anne had been under the care of an orthopedic specialist due to persistent arthritis and rheumatism. His advice to her was that she not become pregnant because it would further complicate her condition. Anne and David ignored the doctor's advice, and a beautiful son was born to them 2 years after their marriage. Three years later Anne further defied her doctor's instructions and became pregnant once again. The pregnancy went well until the middle of the seventh month. At one of her regular checkups, the gynecologist expressed some concern and asked Anne to have an ultrasound. Nothing conclusive was found, and the pregnancy continued with weekly visits to the doctor.

Three weeks later the doctor ordered another ultrasound and informed Anne and David that severe abnormalities were present in their unborn child. If Anne and David were apprehensive, it was only in the privacy of their home. Anne was very close to her mother and sister, but none of them talked about the problematic, unborn child. Three days before the due date Anne and David's child died in utero.

The baby was delivered by natural means and in the delivery room David held the dead baby, but Anne refused the doctor's request to do the same. Anne apparently was having a hard time admitting that her baby was dead; not holding her dead child showed this. Due to the extensive autopsy that was performed, the funeral was not held until 4 days later. During that time Anne did not openly grieve. When visitors came to see her in the hospital, she acted as if she had only had minor surgery. Anne was discharged from the hospital the day before the funeral.

Anne's father had died 8 years before and was buried in their hometown 200 miles away. Anne's mother tried to insist on the child being buried with the grandfather, and Anne was prepared to accede to her mother's wishes. But David disagreed and gently took over, buying a family plot near his and Anne's home. He spoke to the clergy and requested that they try to help him and Anne with the grief they were experiencing. David is a self-employed business-man who needed to be back to his shop within a week. His work was demanding, and he needed to be in control. He was also concerned about Anne's reaction to the death of their baby. Also, the doctor had warned Anne not to get pregnant—she knew she shouldn't have even tried to have a baby in the first place—and because she ignored his instructions, her baby was dead. Anne blocked all these things from her mind and even ignored the fact that her child had died.

At the minister's suggestion, David asked for and was granted permission to dress the baby in preparation for burial. At the funeral service David was the pallbearer for his son. Anne and David had come to know many young parents through prenatal classes for both their children, and a large number of them attended the funeral. They also served lunch to the mourners fol-lowing the service. At the time of this writing, it has been nearly 6 months since the baby's death. David has been able to carry on his business, to be a father to his son and to be a tremendous support for his wife, who is still suffering from unresolved grief.

CASE 4: CRIB DEATH

Lisa, a very demanding child, was very close to her father. Near Lisa's eighteenth birthday, her father died very suddenly of a heart attack, leaving the young woman in deep depression. Soon after her father's death, she met Nick and they immediately formed an intimate relationship. Within a few months, Lisa became pregnant, and a hurried wedding took place. Lisa's family knew and cared for Nick, but Nick's family didn't know Lisa. The fact that Lisa was noticeably pregnant did not exactly endear her to her new hus-band's family. Lisa and Nick lived in her hometown, and they very rarely saw his family.

Four months after the wedding, a healthy, beautiful child was born, whom they named Elizabeth. Mother and child arrived home from hospital. One week later Elizabeth was found dead in her bassinet.

Lisa began psychiatric treatment, but she did so sporadically, many times failing to keep appointments. Her family felt that no member of their family could ever be "crazy" and did not encour-age her treatment. In order to keep peace in the home, Nick did not insist that she go.

Eleven months after the death of Elizabeth, Adam was born. Lisa's mental condition made her incapable of caring for Adam for more than a few days at a time. Many times Nick would take his son to his parents' house so they could take care of him. About 5 years passed during which Nick tried to balance his responsibility as the breadwinner in a distant city (and his need to be with his now hospitalized wife) with visiting his son. His visits to his son, who was well cared for by his parents, gradually became very sporadic. Lisa slowly regained her mental health, but all attempts to regain possession of her son were met with nothing but hostility from the grandparents.

The grandfather was now retired and encouraged Adam in sports; in fact, it became an obsession with him that Adam become a professional athlete. The motivating force behind the grandfather's behavior was to "show" Nick what he missed by "not caring for his son."

Lisa and Nick now have two younger daughters and are a happy, outgoing family with a stable future. They appear at Nick's family functions when necessary, but the lack of friendliness displayed by Nick's parents, brothers and sisters was obviously a barrier to their full participation in the family as a group.

There are many "losers" in this situation. Nick's parents have 21 grandchildren that are measured by their perception that Adam is the "norm" in all aspects. Adam is the biggest "loser." His every desire has been fulfilled—a car; liberal amounts of spending money; he was easily excused when he didn't make the grade as an athlete; he graduated from a community college, with a lot of assistance by relatives who were in the teaching profession. For example, his uncle would pull "all nighters" typing Adam's assignments while Adam slept. He was assisted by his college in procuring jobs, but refused them because they took him away from his support system—his family.

Adam has recently married and has a position in a firm managed by a friend of his wife's father. He has been given every reason to believe that he will get what he wants—in fact, that it will be given to him.

In the mid-1960s, care and support for victims of sudden infant death syndrome was not as advanced as it is today. Even now help is available only to those who seek it. This case was written to show the ongoing effects of one instance of mismanaged or unassisted grief from SIDS.

CASE 5: A 3-YEAR-OLD CHILD WITH CANCER

Jeff and Melissa had been involved in a relationship together since they were in their mid teens. They lived in a large city in a drug-oriented neighborhood. Drug and alcohol use and illicit sex were all normal behavior. After trying many partners, they finally decided to set up housekeeping together—each contributing what they could to their needs by working at whatever jobs were available. Drugs and alcohol, however, had first call on their financial resources.

Nearly a year into the relationship, Melissa became pregnant and almost immediately began seeking help to get her life in order. Through contact with the telephone counseling service of a major television evangelistic ministry, she was referred to a local church. After mild resistance, Jeff joined Melissa in attending church. The members were supportive throughout Melissa's pregnancy and the birth of Natalie. Shortly before Natalie's second birthday, she was diagnosed as having terminal cancer and was given 3 to 6 months to live. Jeff became very bitter, returned to his old bad habits and soon lost his job. Up to this point both Jeff and Melissa's parents were not supportive of their children's life style—their drug use and their religious beliefs. However, they were able to realize the desperate need of this young family. Neither were able to offer much monetary assistance, but Jeff's father owned a farm with an empty house in need of repair, and they asked Jeff and Melissa to move in.

Soon after moving to the farm, Melissa and Jeff began attending a small, country church. Melissa continued to work and Jeff cared for Natalie. The minister and congregation "adopted" the young family and added their moral support and prayers to those of the extended family. The minister went with Melissa to her employer and was successful in obtaining for her an indefinite leave of absence from her job. During the remaining 2 months of Natalie's life, all their needs were supplied by the church. In late November the Sunday School held a Christmas party for Natalie. Natalie enjoyed herself immensely, but after everyone had gone, she told the "preacher lady," "they only did it because I am sick."

Eight days before Christmas, Natalie died peacefully in her mother's arms at home. Melissa and Jeff asked the doctor not to call the funeral director to come for the body. They gave Natalie a bath, dressed her in her best clothes, wrapped her in a blanket and took her to the funeral home. On two occasions they spent time alone with their daughter before the funeral. The only item supplied by the municipality was the wholesale cost of the coffin. All other expenses, including the cemetery plot, the funeral director's services and labor to open and close the grave, were a gift of the community.

The only obstacle to the normal grieving process was the guilt Melissa and Jeff experienced because of their previous life styles.

They were convinced that drug abuse was the cause of their child's disease and, when pressed for an answer, their doctor informed them that it was a possibility. The night before the funeral, Melissa and Jeff knelt in prayer to ask for forgiveness, and through the assurance of the minister, accepted pardon without question. The assistance and support of the community eased the burden and facilitated the grieving process before, during and after the death of their daughter. Two years have passed, Melissa and Jeff have moved to an area where Jeff has found employment, and they are excited about the imminent arrival of the second child.

CASE 6: AN 18-YEAR-OLD ADOLESCENT WITH CANCER

Paula was 37 years old when her husband died of brain cancer. It was a matter of only 3 weeks from the onset of his violent headaches until he died. Paula was a Christian of the fundamentalist bent who believed that grief and mourning meant a lack of faith. So, on the surface, Paula breezed through the following year. If she became depressed, several friends were available to divert her attention from anything that hurt.

About 14 months after her husband's death, Paula's son, Sam, was diagnosed as having cancer of the spine. From the time of diagnosis, Paula resigned herself to the fact that her son would die. She visited him regularly in the hospital and in no way allowed him to see or hear her opinion on his chances of survival.

After active treatment Sam was allowed to go home, and Paula cared for him. She never tired of entertaining the constant stream of young friends from school and church. Sam was considered a model patient by his mother because he was cheerful and outgoing at all times. He played a game with his medication that he called "chicken." His doctor had prescribed medication for pain management on an "as needed" basis; however, Sam would permit himself to get to the point of agony before taking the medication. His mother encouraged him in this game and bragged about it to her friends. Her minister and a friend who was a student minister attempted to counsel Paula and Sam but were met with indifference. The only time Paula allowed herself to be angry was when some people from the church arrived at the door with a message. They claimed the message was from God, and it said that God would heal her son if she would repent of past sins. This alienated her from the church, but she kept in close contact with those who admired her and Sam's stoicism.

Paula would occasionally take time off and go away for a couple of days. Sam's two sisters would care for him, and this was a saving grace for Paula.

About 10 days before Sam died, Paula insisted that he go to the hospital, much against his wishes. She confided to the student minister that she could no longer cope with the increasing amount of care Sam needed. Money was not a problem, and Sam suggested that they hire a nurse, but Paula was dead set against this. Just the inconvenience of a hospital bed in the livingroom had become too much for her to handle. She had put up with Sam's demand that he be allowed to watch television whenever he wanted to, but now she needed to get back to normal.

When Sam went to hospital, he no longer could play his "medication" game because the nurses insisted that he take his medication regularly. Visiting hours were unlimited, but Paula only visited twice a day for an hour at a time. Sam gave up very quickly and died about a week later.

Sam's funeral was a copy of his father's. Paula exhibited almost an air of celebration during the funeral and also in the weeks that followed. She sold her home, put her furniture in storage and went to Hawaii with the group Youth with a Mission. After the initial 3-month training period, she traveled to the Philippines and Japan. This carefree behavior continued for 2 years until an accident—although minor in itself—led to Paula's complete mental breakdown. She was brought home under sedation, with a nurse in attendance. Paula spent several months in a psychiatric hospital and remained under the care of a psychiatrist for almost 3 years. During this period her father and one of her brothers died. With the constant care of the doctor, she was able to begin resolving the compounded grief she had accumulated from the multiple major losses she had undergone.

At the present time, 8 years after the death of her husband, Paula is becoming a whole person. She is beginning to realize that even Jesus wept at the death of his friend.

CASE 7: THE SUICIDE OF A 40-YEAR-OLD MAN

Millie would be 80 years old the following week, and family and friends had planned a community birthday party for her. She knew about the party and was looking forward to having a good time.

Millie was a devout Christian and well respected in the community—but it had not always been that way. For many years she was looked upon as "poor Millie." Her husband was an alcoholic and together they had 11 children in 20 years. Due to the chaotic home environment, six of their children were constantly in trouble with the law and several of them also have drinking problems.

Millie's husband died 30 years before, and Millie was finally able to be her own person. She worked for nearly 20 years before retiring, and this was enough to get her small house in order. She had the wiring and plumbing updated, the outside of the house painted, and she bought new furniture. She bought new clothes and began to take pride in her appearance. The "poor Millie" label disappeared from her neighbors' vocabulary.

At the beginning of the week of her birthday, Millie visited her son, Tim, whose second marriage had just broken up. Tim was very depressed, but Millie felt that in time he would be all right. Tim explained to his mother that he felt bad going to her birthday party without his wife, but aside from that there were no further indications that Tim was terribly depressed.

Two days later Tim's body was discovered in his truck, which was parked in his garage—suicide by carbon monoxide poisoning.

Millie's main concern was for the two sons Tim had from his first marriage. She was able to carry herself extremely well during the time between the death and the funeral, and she consoled the people who came to pay their respects to her son. It was only immediately after the funeral that she asked to see her minister alone. The minister used a modification of the "life review" therapy—taking Millie through the different stages of her life, particularly as they applied to Tim. Neither of them could find any reason for Millie to feel guilty about the quality of her role as a mother. She did weep over the tragedy of her bad marriage but was able to accept her children's behavior as normal in light of the circumstances.

Millie was anxious to put what remained of her unresolved grief on hold because she wanted to have a good time at the birthday party that was being held for her the following day. She did this with great dignity and integrity, in the midst of 200 friends. However, once the party was over, she allowed herself to experience the grief she was feeling. The minister saw her once a week for approximately 6 weeks and then gradually lengthened the time between visits. Millie has since successfully picked up the pieces of her life—as she had done on so many occasions before. The death of her son did not consume her with grief because she had developed an inner strength when it came to facing tragedies—a resource she had built up over the years. A loving, caring community assisted her in the process.

CASE 8: TWO SONS OF A 90-YEAR-OLD WOMAN

Ida had been a resident of a nursing home for nearly 10 years and had recently celebrated her ninetieth birthday. According to her one daughter-in-law she had never been a pleasant woman, and she had succeeded in alienating her four children and their spouses repeatedly. Her youngest son, Tom, left home many years before and had resettled in the Midwest. His visits home were very infrequent, the last time being when his father died and his mother moved to a nursing home.

Ida criticized her son to everyone who would listen until she was told by another one of her sons that Tom was terminally ill with cancer. When Ida heard this, she immediately forgot her anger and elevated Tom to the level of sainthood. When he died a few months later, Mary was completely inconsolable.

Within a year tragedy struck once again—her second son died suddenly of a heart attack and Ida was again consumed with grief. This time she reacted, screaming at Tom's new widow that she had killed him. When her daughter-in-law and grandchildren refused to visit her, she made life miserable for everyone else in the nursing home. The nursing home minister and staff did everything possible to try to soothe Ida's rage. Finally the minister confronted Ida with her past attitudes and suggested to her that her inability to cope with the guilt she felt from her past inadequacies was adding to her present pain.

It was a harrowing experience to watch this once belligerent woman finally coming to terms with herself and seeing as others saw her. For approximately 3 weeks Ida sat in her chair and sobbed quietly. She ate when her tray of food was brought to her and allowed herself to be led to the toilet.

The minister and pastoral care workers at the nursing home spent many hours with Ida. When she wouldn't eat, they literally spoon-fed her and they washed her and helped her dress. This expression of unconditional, non-patronizing love was something that Ida had never experienced before, and she began to respond positively. By the time 6 months passed, Ida became a very different person. The volunteers continued their support but gradually reduced their assistance to avoid a situation in which Ida would become too dependent on them.

By the first anniversary of her second son's death Ida had become a reasonably pleasant person who was able to interact well with other members of the nursing home. The true test of her new attitude came when she got a new roommate who was blind. Ida became her friend and constant companion. Twice during the following year other residents lost children and Ida tried to help them. It has taken a long time for her family to forgive her, but with the help of the minister even that is beginning to happen.

DISCUSSION

After reading most of the literature in the bibliography at the end of this chapter, it is my sense that the age of the child is a factor in the intensity of a parent's grief. The cases cited in this chapter do not, however, bear that out. In the case of an adult child, the parents are often forgotten as all sympathy is given to deceased's spouse and children. As far as I am concerned, it does not matter if the deceased is a grandparent; they are still children to the parents and the loss is just as unnatural.

An issue that may be uncomfortable for some parents to admit is that they fear the death of their child because it would mean they would be losing someone who could be supportive to them in their old age. This would be particularly important to elderly parents who have become dependent on the emotional support from the child who died (as was true in case 8).

Responses to loss may vary depending on age, religion and previous experiences with loss. Also, the quality of the relationship before it ended makes a difference, and everyone has different needs as far as the level of support they require is concerned. Third, the nature and meaning of loss differ with individuals—for example, siblings do not respond to loss of another in the same way.

It is relevant to note that there are unique issues that come with the loss of a fetus, a stillbirth or the death of an infant. From the moment of conception, there are positive and negative feelings attached to the child. Mothers quickly form a bond with a child because they feel the child growing inside them. As the fetus develops in the womb and the body changes occur and movements can be felt, the father, too, will usually participate more actively in his bonding with the unborn child (Rando 1984).

Normal grief symptoms can be expected after a miscarriage. Guilt is a common feeling even more so than anger or frustration. The couple needs to share their fantasies, thoughts and feelings about the unborn child in order to complete the mourning process. In the case of stillbirth it is difficult for the woman to return home after hospitalization for she has nothing to show for her many months of "work" and for all the changes her body went through. While the baby had been very much a part of the lives of the mother and family, it did not even exist for others. This tends to isolate the parents and family from the much needed outside support.

There are five different and unique features of a SIDS (sudden infant death syndrome) loss that complicate the grief and actually victimize the parents and family members:

- *Suddenness:* There was absolutely no opportunity to prepare for the loss.
- *Absence of a Definite Cause:* This prevents a complete definition of the situation by family and caregivers and consequently increases the likelihood of intense guilt, since parents have no reason to feel blameless. Other people can increase their doubts by criticism of the quality of parental care.
- *Problematic Grief Reactions:* When a young child dies, the intense and critical mother-infant bond is abruptly severed. This, plus the possibility that such a loss is the first experience with death that many young married couples encounter, creates an extremely intense and harsh grief experience for the mother. There are similar problems with the father-infant bond for many men. Although they may be less involved physically with the child at this point than mothers are, they still suffer greatly from the loss of a child.
- *Sibling Bereavement:* Siblings suddenly must struggle with guilt over the ambivalent feelings they had about their sibling. Additionally, they are forced to cope with the disruption that their parents' own grief creates for the family.
- *Legal System Involvement:* When the death of a child is sudden and of no known cause, families are forced to deal with police, medical examiners and hospital personnel who must protect the interests of the child and the state by investigating such deaths. However, there is often an insinuation that the death was caused by some act of commission or omission on the part of the families, which places an additional burden of guilt and pain on them (Rando 1984).

A person can lose a child from any other cause and be allowed to grieve in a normal way, but the person who has made a conscious decision to seek an abortion is in a category all by herself. This element of choice, the widespread social acceptance of the abstract idea of abortion, tends to enhance the use of denial as a defense mechanism. While denial is a typical early reaction to grief, it can become so sustained that grief, mourning and guilt are never dealt with.

CONCLUSION

There are many variables in dealing with grief after the loss of a child. From the foregoing cases it becomes obvious that those who have experienced support in a tangible way are better able to cope. Those who have even one significant other to be there for them will come through the process with the least amount of permanent damage. There would appear to be little difference in the ages of the parents or of the children. A major difference would appear to be their openness in being ministered to, both spiritually and emotionally.

The sudden upsurge of interest in learning about how to minister to those who are dying and to the bereaved is a step in the right direction. However, the first step must be that each person comes to grips with her own mortality. We must realize that we cannot own another human being—they are a gift for a certain time and then we must let go. To live in readiness to let go must be our goal no matter what the relationship. When this comes for us then we can be instruments to facilitate the process for others.

REFERENCES

Adams, David W., and Deveau, Eleanor J. *Coping with Childhood Cancer.* Reston, VA: Reston Publishing Company, 1984.

Adams-Greenly, Margaret. Communicating about serious illness and death. *J. Psychol. Oncology* 1(1), 1984.

Bordow, Joan. *The Ultimate Loss: Coping with the Death of a Child.* New York: Beaufort Books, 1944.

Cook, Judith A. Influence of gender on the problems of parents of fatally ill children. *J. Psychol. Oncology* 1(1), 1984.

Gentles, Ian, ed. *Care for the Dying and the Bereaved.* Toronto: Anglican Book Centre, 1982.

Kübler-Ross, Elisabeth. *On Children and Death.* New York: Macmillan, 1983.

———. *On Death and Dying.* New York: Macmillan, 1969.

Lang, Gordon. A method for doing grief work with families who have had a child die of cancer. *J. Pastoral Care* 38(1), 1984.

Lewis, C. S. *A Grief Observed.* New York: Benton, 1961.

Rando, Theresa A. *Grief, Dying and Death.* Champaign, IL: Research Press, 1984.

Richards, Larry and Johnson, Paul. *Death and the Caring Community.* Portland, OR: Multnormah Press, 1980.

Schiff, Harriett Sarnoff. *The Bereaved Parent.* London: Penguin Books, 1977.

Yarwood, Anne. *Losing a Baby.* Ottawa: The Canadian Institute of Child Health, 1983.

14

The Sudden Death of a Child: Crisis Intervention from a Medical Investigator's Office

Carol Chapin, BSN, MA

It should not hurt to be a parent, but it often does. When a child dies, parents are confronted with a situation that is perhaps more devastating than anyone could imagine. This agonizing experience can be even worse when death occurs suddenly and unexpectedly. In the state of New Mexico, 500 to 600 children die suddenly each year, throwing families into profound and crippling pain. This chapter will discuss the crisis intervention system that has been established in New Mexico.

When a child dies after a long illness—when death is antici- pated at some point in the near or far future, parents will suffer greatly from the loss, but perhaps there is also some sense of relief; the child no longer has to suffer and the parents no longer have to stand by helplessly and watch the terrible process of death. But when children die unexpectedly—by suicide, homicide, accidents, or unexplained natural causes—families are thrown into crisis in the most pronounced sense of the word.

Families in a crisis of this dimension require intervention. The New Mexico Office of the Medical Investigator (OMI) offers a pro- gram of rapid, informed intervention for families who experience the unexpected death of a child. The OMI deals only with those deaths that are reported through their office—deaths that are sud- den and unexpected. Known as the New Mexico Grief Intervention Program (GIP), it immediately makes crisis counseling available as needed and as requested by families.

The OMI team is composed of forensic pathologists, investigators, autopsy staff, and grief counselors. In addition, the team is assisted by a statewide network of volunteers who are health professionals and bereaved parents themselves. The volunteers are an integral part of the program and are trained by our staff counselors. A detailed discussion of volunteer procedures and qualifications is provided later in this chapter. Because of immediate access to computer data of reports of death, information regarding cause and manner of death (as determined by the forensic staff), and the ability to locate surviving family members, grief counselors are in a strategic position to provide intervention. Moreover, grief counselors have "legitimate" access to homes, thus making the job of assisting those families that they feel are in a state of siege much easier.

DAILY ROUTINE

The grief intervention staff's daily routine begins with a review of the computer printout of the deaths of children aged 1 through 18 that have occurred since the previous day. Staff counselors attend morning report to view the bodies of children who have died in the previous 24 hours. There are various benefits of seeing the child after death: we can learn something about the child just by seeing him and this provides us with a sense of relatedness with the family. When they know we have seen their child, they feel closer to us and believe that we can answer questions: Did he die suddenly, or did he suffer? Was her face intact? Why can't I see his body? You saw her; isn't her hair beautiful? Going through this process—reviewing the deaths that occurred and actually viewing the bodies—gives us a chance to approach the situation as a team, and this gives us the benefit of receiving everyone's input. We also begin to get an understanding of the cause and manner of death, and this, too, prepares us to answer the many questions parents inevitably ask.

Morning routine includes writing and sending a condolence letter to all new families along with grief material appropriate to individual causes of death—whether suicide, homicide, accident, or disease. This letter tells the family how to contact a pathologist, counselor, or volunteer and how to join a support group in their area. If the family resides within 50 miles of the central office in Albuquerque, an initial telephone call is made to offer a visit, make an assessment of any needs the family may have, and perhaps listen to a parent talk or cry. This early contact can help to allay some of the anxieties of grief, answer questions, and help families begin to tackle the confusing and painful grief process.

Computer report data and autopsy findings give counselors the ability to answer the many questions parents have. Finding out exactly how and, if possible, why a loved one died can be an important element in starting the healing process. It also prevents parents from hiding in denial. Most parents cannot stop asking why, and many have a hard time accepting that death has actually occurred and is final until these questions have been answered—and even when they have, death is hard to face. Counselors do their best to provide answers to all the questions parents have, but obviously there are not answers to all questions. Perhaps their inner turmoil will diminish when they can accept this fact. The more questions pathologists and counseling staff can answer early on, the faster a parent can proceed to other aspects of the grief process. We can provide answers to almost all of the questions regarding physical aspects of the death—whether the child died rapidly and whether he or she suffered. Fortunately, the answer to the latter question is usually no.

After the initial call, a home visit is attempted as soon as possible. When a death has just occurred, the family is frequently surrounded by many people (for example, the extended family or members of their church). Because of this sudden and sometimes constant onslaught of people, they may be hesitant or not as anxious to accept the help of outsiders. It is also understandable that immediately following a death, families will not want to meet one more stranger; after all, their lives have been intruded upon by the police, emergency medical technicians, investigators, and probably an assortment of other people—all of whom have wormed their way into their lives, which by this point usually have taken on the quality of a terrible nightmare. Generally, after a couple of weeks have elapsed, when the initial shock of death wanes and the actual reality of the situation—the pain, loneliness, and fear—becomes clear, families may be more amenable to the idea of allowing a grief counselor to assist them.

VISITING THE BEREAVED FAMILY AT HOME

The home visit consists of an assessment of the current emotional and physical reactions of the surviving family members; we discuss how they are feeling at that moment and try to anticipate what they should expect to feel in the future; we provide education about the grieving process with information about what seemed to help other parents, as well as suggesting appropriate educational materials; we offer referrals to relevant support groups and other community resources; finally, we do the best we can to fully answer as many of their questions as possible.

Many parents ask, "Did my child really kill herself?" The police report and the pathologist may tell them yes, but that answer is often simply unacceptable to some parents; they find it very hard to believe that their child was miserable enough to commit suicide. Also, it is terribly painful for parents to accept that their child would do something that would have such awful repercussions for their families. Another common question is "How could that condition have killed my child?" Certain causes of death can be hard for parents to comprehend—for example, when a baby dies of sudden infant death syndrome (SIDS) and there are essentially no autopsy findings; when meningitis or myocarditis is preceded only by minor sniffles just before death; or when everyone in a car accident survives and their child dies. Understandably, parents feel anger at life's unfairness and experience intense confusion after a sudden death.

It is important to keep the contacts with bereaved parents going and to reassess the family situation and problems as they occur. There are very few people who are willing to listen to a story of death told over and over again or to a parent's depression, anger, or guilt. We try to fulfill as many needs as possible and to provide as much listening time as we can.

We have also found that other family members may need special attention. Grandparents, for example, are dealt a double blow—they've lost a grandchild and also have to learn to live with the pain their own child is now immersed in. Siblings report that the death of a brother or sister leaves a hole in their lives that is never completely filled. They suffer the loss of intimacy they had with the person they shared their entire childhood with; the loss of someone they knew in a way they will never know another person; the loss of a special support system—support they may not even receive from their spouse, best friend, or parents. When a brother or sister dies, the surviving sibling suddenly experiences the realization of his own mortality: "If it can happen to him, it can happen to me." This can cause intense fear, and counselors should always be aware of this possibility, making careful assessments during home visits. All siblings seen by program staff or volunteers should always be referred to appropriate support groups.

VOLUNTEERS

New Mexico, one of the largest states geographically, has many remote and poorly accessible areas, as well as a culturally diverse population. Because of this, it is difficult for us to have contact with and to provide grief assistance to families in areas that are far from the central office. For this reason, we use community volunteers who allow us to reach many families that would otherwise go unaided. Community volunteer contact provides families with personal, face-to-face support and also gives staff at the central office a better evaluation of the family situation and needs which otherwise might not be discernible through telephone reach-out alone. GIP volunteers are an essential part of the crisis intervention team, offering direct, hands-on services to families in their time of greatest need.

When a family resides in an outlying area, a volunteer should be contacted by the GIP office. The volunteer should be given all information that is available about the particular family. The volunteer should then be asked if he or she is willing to try to help the family. Volunteers should be properly suited to families in terms of their geographical location, their age, and of paramount importance, their personal knowledge of the repercussions caused by different forms of death and how to confront the issues relative to each. Perinatal death carries with it different problems than, say, suicide. Once volunteers have accepted a "job," they are instructed to call the family they have been assigned to. Sometimes volunteers are turned away by the family—for reasons explained earlier—but in time (usually about 2 weeks) most families become more agreeable to accepting assistance. Volunteers should always make a second call, especially if they were turned away the first time; we know that this is a normal reaction and doesn't necessarily mean that the family will not need and want help later; as we have seen, family needs can change radically in 2 weeks' time.

If their personalities are compatible and the volunteer has the time, he or she may visit the family as often as both parties want. The type and amount of assistance given by a volunteer depends, of course, on the special needs of the family. At first, a family may require and want more information and help than they will need as time goes by. Volunteers may find that after a while, they no longer have to spend nearly as much time or energy working with the family. It is suggested, however, that after 3 months the volunteer should contact the family, either by mail or phone, or in person.

This should be done again 1 month before the first anniversary of the child's death.

The volunteer network is just one of the statewide resources maintained by the GIP. Contacts have been developed throughout the state with bereavement support groups, mental health centers, schools and churches with bereavement programs, and psychologists and counselors who specialize in the many different aspects of grief work. At the family's request, we will make referrals to the Crime Victims Reparation Commission, the New Mexico Victims Assistance Organization, Parents of Murdered Children, Mothers Against Drunk Driving, Survivors of Suicide, and other agencies that provide crisis, legal, educational, and financial assistance. Finally, we have a network of contact persons and programs on Pueblo, Navajo, and Apache Indian lands.

Grief work can be extremely stressful. Workers in the field are faced with a daily reminder of their own mortality, as well as the very real fact that their children, too, might die an unexpected death. They are involved in the intense and dramatic pain of others; this objective view is particularly distressing and hard to face. Perhaps, when experiencing something as awful as the death of their own child, a parent's life can assume a bizarre, unreal quality, but when viewed objectively, when the pain is seen happening to someone else, it sometimes hurts in a more graphic way—an emotion that can be extraordinarily painful. Also, when counselors become familiar with the many problems that a death can cause in a family, they often are able to anticipate traumatic situations such as divorce, neglect of surviving children, and other problems; this, too, is a hard part of this job. We are moved by all families in pain, but sometimes a particularly tragic or horrible death can really hit home. There is no question that grief counseling takes a high toll on one's emotions. Because of the high price we must pay for doing work of this sort, it is essential for us to take measures to maintain a balanced and sane frame of mind. One important task is to debrief each other as soon as possible after family and group contacts. This can range from a word or two to simply touch base to a blow-by-blow account, depending on each situation. Debriefing can be especially necessary when the situation is particularly painful for staff. Tears are never prohibited; in fact, because crying—actually showing the emotions one is experiencing—is so important, tears are a normal, if not necessary event, both in the office and shared with bereaved families. To alleviate stress we exercise whenever possible—at work.

We also have our own brand of humor. There are jokes that revolve around every job; our jokes might be considered tasteless by others but we sometimes need to view our sad experiences with a bit of humor.

In spite of the pain we encounter and the swirl of devastating emotions that we get caught up in, there is joy in knowing that we can help; we know that we cannot stop or end the terrible pain that bereaved families experience, but we can assuage it. Healing does occur at some point, and knowing that we can be part of that process is important to us. Involvement by a group such as ours can help the family to avoid unnecessary pitfalls, thereby perhaps shortening the grieving process. There is a visible and rapid change that accompanies intervention and that is a real inspiration to all of us.

CONCLUSION

I strongly believe that it is impossible to do grief work without coming to terms with your own mortality. It is also essential to have a general understanding of the paradox of life; death is part of life and in order to live, death must be faced. Yes, life can seem unfair. It can even be terrible. But there is joy in living and our aim at the GIP is to help bereaved families understand this.

15

A Sociological Model for Grieving Parents

Gerry R. Cox, PhD

The purpose of this chapter is to examine the various coping processes that parents grieving over the loss of their child might use. The main hypothesis posed here is that in order to cope with the death of a child, parents have special needs and require specific social adjustment skills that few have when their child dies. This means coping, in some cases, through the whole miserable process of their child's terminal illness, and then the actual death itself. The initial extreme pain that parents experience over the death of their child often won't go away rapidly; it will, however, gradually lessen in its severity and should eventually become at least bearable. I will begin by discussing the numerous coping skills that parents can use to help them get through the terrible ordeal of the death of their child. I will also examine the various pitfalls that many parents encounter—marital problems, for example. Finally, I cover the concept of choice; there is no question that the way we live our lives is a matter of choice, and if this is appreciated, especially in times of disaster, it is easier to face life more realistically and fully. This, in turn, will help parents to deal more successfully with problems as they occur.

One of the most difficult tragedies a person will ever face is the death of a child; this is, without question, an extraordinarily painful experience for a parent. Whether the child dies due to miscarriage, stillbirth, abortion, complications after birth, sudden infant death syndrome, accident or disease, the resulting pain and hurt can be so severe that it is capable of crippling a person emotionally, and sometimes even physically. To cope successfully with this type of disaster requires skills that very few people have ever had a need to develop and even if they have, few are capable of ever mastering them. Certainly, this is not to imply that one shouldn't try. Indeed, the purpose of this chapter is to help parents to learn grieving skills so that they will be able to cope with the death of their child.

COPING

As I have stressed above, the death of a child presents a unique challenge to a parent's coping abilities. Children are by nature an extension of their parents and when a child dies, so, too, does part of the parent. It is also devastating to lose one's parents, but one generally has hopes and dreams for children that are greater and more far-reaching. It is expected that parents will probably die before their children, and as medical technology continues to advance, it is safe to assume that today's children will live longer than their parents did. No matter how many children a couple may have, or how many they plan to have in the future, it is simply impossible to "replace" the child that dies—each child is a special person and cannot be replaced by another.

All children have bonds with their parents, and that binding relationship is unique. The bonding process may begin even before the start of pregnancy. Some parents begin to anticipate and plan long before their child is conceived. For others, bonding begins only after the baby is born. In any case, almost all parents develop a strong bond with their children at one point or another. Even when parents have serious problems with their children, the bond remains. Obviously, the tighter the bond, the more severe is the pain when the child dies. Of course bonding occurs with friends, parents, grandparents, spouses and others, but the bond between parent and child is entirely special, and far more intense.

After the death of a child, life might not seem to be worth living, but this feeling does not last forever. Grief occurs in waves— sometimes it feels overwhelming; other times its severity lessens (Tatellbaum 1980). One does not return to "normal" after a tragedy of this sort, but after the passing of time the hard periods seem to come with less frequency and the good times can once again be felt.

No matter what feeling or emotions one has when grieving, never make the mistake of thinking that your "method" is wrong; whatever you feel, and any way you choose to express these feelings, is appropriate. What is important is that you allow yourself to feel something and let it out in any way you can.

Numerous excellent books have been written on the psychological adjustment needed to cope successfully with the death of a child and what to expect during the grieving process. These include works by DeFrain, Taylor and Ernst (1984); Epstein, Weitz, Walton and Abramowitz (1976); Ezell, Anspaugh and Oaks (1987); Glick, Weiss and Parkes (1974); Westberg (1971); Kastenbaum (1981); Wilcox and Sutton (1981); Schultz (1978); Feifel (1959); and Boerstler (1982). Schneidman (1974, 1980) is particularly helpful with suicide.

In his books written in 1977 and 1980, Earl Grollman has proved especially knowledgeable when it comes to teaching about children. Perhaps the best single book for parents is Elisabeth Kübler-Ross' *Children and Death* (1983), though she has authored numerous other books of considerable value as well. There are many textbooks on the subject of death and dying that provide helpful ideas; they include those by Leming and Dickenson (1985); Stephenson (1985); DeSpelder and Strickland (1987); Charmaz (1980); Kalish (1985); and Smith (1985). A host of literary works have also been published that bear on the subject. While psychological grieving is a private matter, grieving has a social impact on all the groups to which one belongs.

Individual Coping Patterns

When one is grieving for the loss of a child, other relationships will suffer as well. If this is recognized and care is taken, the chance of damaging these relationships will not be as great. Parents often fail to see that their surviving children are also grieving for the lost brother or sister. Children grieve differently than adults, and they do different things when they grieve. Some cry openly, while others take time to think it through, and still others hide in their rooms. The way they grieve is never wrong. Some parents might think that their children are not grieving because they do not seem to be showing any emotion. It must be remembered that every person has their own method of grieving. Children need to be able to grieve in their own way. Children with a brother or sister who has died need time and attention; they need to be included and informed (Stillion 1985). Some children may exhibit extreme emotions, while others seem to have none to show. Children also need to be told how their parents feel so they can better understand the way they are acting (Cutter 1974). The death of a child should never be the occasion for separation from a still living child. A parent should not become too protective of the remaining children or of any future children. They must be allowed to remain free and not be smothered. They need love and care, but they also need to live for themselves. Parents need time away from their children, too. The death of a child should make one a more capable parent, not a diminished one.

Not only can the relationship with a child suffer, but so can the relationship with one's spouse. Spouses do not necessarily grieve in the same way or at the same time. If both spouses work outside the home, the one who returns to work first seems to be the one who is handling the loss better. For some, work is like therapy; it is a way to deal with stresses and to think things through. Each person has a particular way to deal with the problems that occur in life. If work is simply a distraction, then the one who returns to work may simply be delaying the grief. Parents who go to work may feel an emptiness when they get home. Work associates compound the problem by not knowing what to say or do. It is as though the loss never occurred when one is at work, but the pain can be almost overwhelming when one returns home (Edelstein 1984). Differences in the experience of grief are often distressing to relationships and can predispose couples to divorce (Cuttler 1974). Couples need to beware that the death of a child is a great stress on their marriage. By being aware they can take steps to deal with the problem before it gets out of hand.

Grandparents and other relatives and friends can present special problems for bereaved parents. Such persons often seem unable to deal with the grieving process. Many refuse to discuss the problem, pretend that the child never existed, suggest that the parent ought to be "over" the grief, and seem to take the view that nothing ever happened. Successful grieving may include spending considerable time talking about the child who died. That child is still a part of the parents' life. It is healthy to talk about the child. It's okay to mention the child's name. It's okay, too, to cry with the parents.

Caregivers may also contribute to the problems parents have in dealing with the death of their child. Physicians may be uncomfortable with their own feelings about death and may unwittingly cause the parents further pain and contribute to their difficulties in facing the loss (Garfield 1978). Physicians, clergy, social workers and parents of other dying children can all be of help to grieving parents if they have a handle on their own grief.

Parents are typically not prepared to deal with the intense emotions they experience. Social adjustment skills must be developed by parents who have lost a child. It would be far preferable if these skills were developed prior to the tragedy itself.

Coping Skills

Coping skills are needed to deal with all kinds of problems in one's life. One might assume that the death of a child is not all that different in that it is a crisis that one goes through. One also experiences the death of other significant people; people move, lose jobs, have accidents, all of which may produce a crisis. Coping skills are taught to many of those who must deal with the dislocation of a divorce. The skills to deal with the death of a child are a little more difficult to handle than most other losses.

For most parents the biggest obstacle to coping with the loss of a child is that they focus upon what was lost instead of what they had in the relationship with the child. In every relationship there are good times and bad times, but a parent loves a child unconditionally. The love of a child is not based upon correct behavior. When a child dies, the loss should not be based upon unfulfilled wishes and irreversible regrets. One loses the relationship with the child; that is the true loss. That relationship enriched the lives of the child's parents. They must strive to remember the good times and learn to accept the bad.

To cope with the loss of a child, you must remember that others do not grieve as you do. Your parents, friends, neighbors, and even your spouse will grieve differently than you grieve. Your parents may put away pictures of your child and prefer to talk about anything else. Your spouse may return to work and seem to forget. Your friends may change the subject when you bring up the name of your child. Your other children may play or read or simply not leave their rooms. It is not that they do not share your grief. Their way of grieving is simply different than yours. You need to be aware that others cannot feel exactly as you do. It is probably out of their concern for the grief you feel that they change the subject and try to be strong when you are suffering the most. It is often a feeling of helplessness, rather than a lack of caring, that makes some people seem callous.

Someone who has lost a child needs to be prepared for bad days. Grief does not remain at the same level of intensity all the time. Certain days will be worse than others. One can expect that anniversaries, birthdays, holidays and other special days will cause renewed grief. Sometimes, for no apparent reason, one has a bad day. Time is not a healer. These bad days may very well occur for the rest of one's life. The intensity may lessen, but the pain may never go away. Learning to cope, and not time, lessens the intensity of grief.

To cope with the death of a child, one also needs to recognize that the emotions one feels are simply a natural expression. No emotion is wrong per se. The emotion itself is blameless. If one hates the doctors, or even life in general, it may be understandable. To have a momentary feeling of hate is not in itself wrong. One does need to overcome these feelings if they get in the way of living a productive life. To cope, one must eventually forgive and go on with life. Hatred keeps this from occurring. One needs to accept the emotions one experiences as normal and go on from there. To spend a lot of energy trying to analyze emotions has little value. One should accept them and build from that acceptance.

Coping may also require a recognition that one could face problems in marriage. Such problems often occur after the death of a child. Couples often consider divorce after such a tragedy (Cutter 1974). The spouses need to recognize that the pain they are experiencing could cause them to draw within rather than sharing and growing through the experience as a couple. Crises often trigger problems in marriages. The death of a child is likely to cause the greatest difficulty because the pain is so intense.

One needs also to recognize that caregivers are certainly not perfect, and many may not be able to give effective help in a time of grief. Other caregivers should be sought out: hospice workers, members of Compassionate Friends and other groups may be of considerable help. Someone in one of these groups may well be able to recognize a grieving parent's needs and respond to them.

For many parents the return to work will provide some relief from the pain of the loss. The danger is that such distractions may cause one to overlook the self-examination needed to obtain relief from the distress of grief (Cutter 1974). If the return to work causes excessive loneliness or emptiness, one needs to take the time to try and work through the grief. While at work, associates, clients, customers and others may compound the problem by not knowing what to say or do (Edelstein 1984). It is their avoidance of facing the issue that creates new problems. One does not have to know what to say. Simply being there is often enough. One can only say I'm sorry so many times. The grieving parent is aware of the sorrow. Friends and acquaintances must be willing to listen rather than judge the grieving parent.

It should be recognized that one never really returns to "normal" after the death of a child. Death causes a permanent change. Whether the change is positive or negative depends upon the person. While men seem to adjust better, it is not necessarily true that going to work helps them through their grief more quickly. If anything, the distraction of the job might mean that they take longer to resolve their grief. Recovery is generally slow for mothers who do not work outside the home. They have more time to brood and do not get back into routines as easily. One needs to recognize that the pain will continue. Part of the problem with coping is that the parents are afraid they will forget the child that died (DeFrain 1986). A gnawing sense of guilt may consume them if they do not ease up and allow themselves to go back to living. Their goal in working through grief ought not be to take away the pain of the loss, but rather to go ahead with the idea of living with the loss.

THE LESSON OF DEATH

The most important message of death is what is important in life. If one is not careful, one might begin to think that the newest model car with 1.9% interest is what is really important. Who could afford to pass up such a deal? But what if it means that in making the payments, one must change a whole lifestyle. If one is not careful, one might start thinking that after several seasons of disappointments, the Green Bay Packers may suddenly start winning. Would that change the course of the universe—or of a single life?

Obviously, people all too often are not careful. It is easy to be sidetracked about what is important. One sometimes feels that "this is it!" Yet new cars, winning sports teams, vacations, awards and recognition by others will not suffice. Such things are not bad; they simply do not satisfy real human needs. Such things can enhance one's life and can make it better, or they can serve as a distraction that contributes nothing. When someone dies and one's mother, father, wife, husband, son or daughter is placed in a casket, the car one drives, the Green Bay Packers' record, the home one lives in, the club one belongs to, and the recognition one receives are somehow not nearly so important.

Death is not an easy lesson, but it is a lesson. It hurts when someone we really love dies. The hurt will never truly end. It will become bearable, and life will go on, but things will never be the same. And yet there is wisdom to be gained from the hurt. The death of another causes one to stop the merry-go-round and to think about what is of value and what is really important. Is a genuine smile from a real friend worth more than having thousands of fans seeking autographs? Is taking two strokes off your golf game worth more than an hour with your children on a Sunday? Is money given to aid another worth more than leaving a large bank account when you die?

Death is a gift to the living. It can give them a new lease on life. Each person has a unique contribution to make. Some may teach more by their failures and lost purpose in life; others may teach by example. Good teachers must live what they teach. One may teach in the classroom or in the gutter. Everyone learns from others, and everyone has much to teach to others. Do we teach others to die from cocaine? Do we teach them to love their children as we have loved our children? Is our way of dealing with life teaching others to complain and to prophesy doom? Our deeds teach others even when we do not see ourselves as teachers.

Sociologist William Isaac Thomas noted that all people define their situations. Thomas' concept of "definition of the situation" suggests that we define our families, marriages, jobs, friends and associates (Thomas 1923). This is a continual and never-ending process. Each person has the ability to make his life miserable or happy. One can define the world as a dirty, evil place or as a challenge to make better, or any other definition one may choose. A person can be troubled with herself and those around her, or she can look for the good in herself and those around her. A person can choose to allow others to make him angry or sad, or utterly dejected. No one can actually make you angry. You choose to let them make you angry. By learning to be fully conscious of his actions, a person can take full control of his life. If he does not learn to make decisions and to take control, a person simply drifts along like a fisherman's bobber in the stream, allowing every twist or turn of the stream to control his life. The person becomes weak and helpless and a slave to the whims of others who manipulate him like the bobber in the stream. Some may delude themselves into thinking that they can control their lives without making decisions—but does the cork control the fisherman? By letting others define her, the individual tends to fulfill their prophecies. The concept of self-fulfilling prophecy suggests that unless one takes control, he will live up to the definitions or labels that others place on him. Because teachers, parents, friends and associates define them as inferior, many individuals go through life believing that they can't do those things that they might very well be able to do. By making the effort to examine himself carefully, a person can then decide what he really can do. How many students find excuses not to study for a test because they fear that they will do poorly regardless of whether they study? The result is a lower self-concept.

How many of us worry about what other people think of us in a busy airport even though we will probably never see any of these people again? By making our own decisions about self-worth, we can free ourselves of reliance on the opinions of others. If nothing else, we can have less anxiety over what other people think. We can then live the life and the lifestyle that we choose for ourselves rather than behaving as others expect us to.

If we are able to live the type of life and lifestyle we choose, facing death becomes much easier. Too many people are filled with regrets and "if onlys." If you live the life you choose to live, then there will be fewer regrets when you finally face your own impending death. Perhaps you would like to live to see who wins the Superbowl or the World Series, but if you have followed your own road instead of the road that others would have you follow, you will be content that you have lived your life. Each person must pursue a particular dream. Don't say, "someday." If you have a dream, follow it. Each person can find purpose or meaning in life if he can pursue what he really wants from life. The goals that others encourage one to follow are their dreams and not yours. Society tells the individual to work for fame, fortune, big houses and success. If that is not what you really want for your life, then you will not be satisfied if you follow what society says. If you spend all your time getting rich, you may not get to know and love your own children. You may not write your book or make your mark. Time can never really be wasted, but it can be used in ways that leave one with deep regrets. You only have so much time, and you must decide how to use that time. As a parent, you can choose to use it to make money for your children, or simply to be with your children. If you have made the choice to spend your life with people, your grieving can be better dealt with when any of those people die. In the end, it is not how long you have to spend with another person, but rather the quality of time that you spend with him.

REFERENCES

Boerstler, Richard W. *Letting Go: A Holistic and Meditative Approach to Living and Dying.* South Yarmouth, MA: Associates in Thanatology, 1982.

Charmaz, Kathy. *The Social Reality of Death: Death in Contemporary America.* Reading, MA: Addison-Wesley, 1980.

Cutter, Fred. *Coming to Terms with Death: How to Face the Inevitable with Wisdom and Dignity.* Chicago: Nelson-Hall, 1974.

DeFrain, John, Leona Martens, Jan Stork, and Warren Stork. *Stillborn: The Invisible Death.* Lexington, MA: Lexington Books, 1986.

DeFrain, John, Jacque Taylor, and Linda Ernst. *Coping with Sudden Infant Death.* Lexington, MA: D.C. Heath, 1984.

DeSpelder, Lynne Ann, and Albert Lee Strickland. *The Last Dance: Encountering Death and Dying.* Palo Alto, CA: Mayfield, 1987.

Edelstein, Linda. *Maternal Bereavement: Coping with the Unexpected Death of a Child.* New York: Praeger, 1984.

Epstein, Gerald M., Lawrence J. Weitz, Barbara S. Wallston, and Stephen I. Abramowitz. Professionals' preference for support systems for the bereaved family. *J. Commun. Psychol.* 4(1):69–73, 1976.

Feifel, Herman (ed.). *The Meaning of Death.* New York: McGraw-Hill, 1959.

Glick, Ira O., Robert S. Wiss, and C. Murray Parkes. *The First Year of Bereavement.* New York: John Wiley, 1974.

Kalish, Richard A. *Death, Grief, and Caring Relationships.* Monterey, CA: Brooks/Cole, 1985.

Kastenbaum, Robert J. *Death, Society, and Human Experience.* St. Louis: C. V. Mosby, 1981.

Kübler-Ross, Elisabeth. *On Death and Dying.* New York: Macmillan, 1969.

———. *Questions and Answers on Death and Dying.* New York: Macmillan, 1974.

———. *Death: The Final Stage of Growth.* Englewood Cliffs, NJ: Prentice Hall, 1975.

———. *To Live Until We Say Good-bye.* Englewood Cliffs, NJ: Prentice Hall, 1975.

———. *On Children and Death.* New York: Collier, 1983.

Leming, Michael R., and George E. Dickenson. *Understanding Dying, Death, and Bereavement.* New York: Holt, Rinehart & Winston, 1985.

Schultz, Richard. *The Psychology of Death, Dying, and Bereavement.* Reading, MA: Addison-Wesley, 1978.

Schneidman, Edwin S. *Death of Man.* Baltimore: Penguin Books, 1974.

———. *Death: Current Perspectives.* Palo Alto, CA: Mayfield, 1980.

Smith, Walter J. *Dying in the Human Life Cycle: Psychological, Biomedical, and Social Perspectives.* New York: Holt, Rinehart & Winston, 1985.

Stephenson, John S. *Death, Grief, and Mourning: Individual and Social Realities.* New York: Free Press, 1985.

Stillion, Judith M. *Death and the Sexes: An Examination of Differential Longevity, Attitudes, Behaviors, and Coping Skills.* Washington, DC: Hemisphere, 1985.

Thomas, William I. *The Unadjusted Girl.* Boston: Little, Brown, 1923.

Westberg, Granger E. *Good Grief: A Constructive Approach to the Problem of Loss.* Philadelphia: Fortress Press, 1971.

Wilcox, Sandra Galdieri, and Marilyn Sutton. *Understanding Death and Dying: An Interdisciplinary Approach.* Sherman Oaks, CA: Alfred, 1987.

16

Paternal Response to the Death of an Older Child

Dennis E. Saylor, PhD

In a sense all people are children in that all have a biological mother and father and though all persons are children, it is obvious that not all children become parents. But once a person becomes a mother or father their relationship to that child is permanent. In other words, once a parent always a parent. No matter what chronological age a child may be, the parent and child have a biological and historical relationship.

It follows, then, that any traumatic event—terminal illness or sudden death, for example—that occurs to a child at any age will impact upon the parents of that child. Even though the child may be past adolescence, or even past middle age, the emotional impact of such a trauma will be no less on the parents.

Since the loss of a child at any age, for any reason, has such a profound emotional effect upon the parents, further examination is warranted. In this chapter, attention will be directed to the biological father of the child, rather than on the parents as a couple. This is not to imply that a mother or an adoptive father would respond differently; it is only to identify a specific population for study. Further focus will be upon children in their twenties. Again, this is to delineate a given group, and no case is made that fathers would respond differently to the loss of a younger or older child.

Children at various ages of life have various mortality rates and will succumb to different causes of death. This chapter will examine children's mortality from four causes: accident, suicide, cancer and AIDS. They have been chosen because they are the likely causes of death for the age category being considered.

ACCIDENTAL DEATH

Between the ages of 15 to 24, accidental death claimed the lives of 48.5 young people per 100,000 population. The following case history concerns a 23-year-old girl who was the eldest of four children. She died in surgery following an auto accident in which her vehicle skidded off the road on an icy overpass of an interstate highway. The accident occurred in November 1983.

Her father, Mr. A., is a corporate executive with considerable responsibility. Mr. A. had been in military service as a pilot in the Navy. He was one of two children and as a youngster suffered the death of his brother. Because of this event he was determined to have more than two children of his own. Also during his youth several other close relatives had died. His military training gave him a realization of the fragility of life and, paradoxically, a sense of his own immortality.

On the night of the accident, Mr. A. was concerned about his daughter's late arrival home and had called the state police inquiring about reported accidents. The call he received subsequently from the emergency room physician was, nevertheless, still a great shock—his daughter was in the hospital, critically injured after a car accident. Based on what the hospital told him, he didn't think that his daughter would live until he and his wife could travel the nearly 200 miles to the hospital where she had been taken.

Mr. A. reported to us that the most difficult aspect of the tragedy at this point was conveying the news to his wife, a nurse on duty; handling her distress and dealing with her emotional breakdown was the hardest part of the ordeal, he said.

They immediately drove to the hospital where their daughter had been taken, but were delayed by yet another accident on the same interstate. Ironically, Mr. A. reported at that time feeling an unusual calm and sense of release during this period on the highway. It was at about that same time that their daughter died.

In our interview some 4 years following this tragedy, Mr. A. was able to articulate the events and his feelings very openly and with great sensitivity. He enumerated several things that he felt enabled him to cope and the things that were helpful to him during his grieving process.

1. His daughter's injuries were so profound that even if she had lived, the quality of her life would have been unacceptable. His knowledge of brainstem injury and intercranial

bleeding made him realize that her ability to be fully functional would be forever lost. He did not want her to exist in
that state.

2. Another source of help was the realization that her injuries
   had been instantaneous and, therefore, she experienced no
   suffering or pain. She had not, indeed could not, have
   regained consciousness at any time. This, too, was comforting.

3. Comfort was also derived from the quality of their relationship. Although the daughter had been a "difficult" child to
   raise, Mr. A. recalled a conversation his daughter and wife
   had had just 2 weeks before her death. She confided to her
   mother that "for the first time, I'm beginning to like who I
   am." This self-acceptance conveyed to her father a sense of
   completeness and maturity which she had sought and had
   found at last.

4. Because of his close encounters with risk and danger as a
   pilot and the early deaths of his brother and other relatives,
   Mr. A. felt that he had a somewhat unique perspective on
   death; death may occur but "life goes on"—what can't be
   controlled should be accepted. Realizing that he would
   never "get over" his daughter's death—that she was forever
   irreplaceable, Mr. A. acknowledged that the passing of time
   helped ease the acute pain of the loss.

5. Great strength and comfort were derived from his own personal faith: quoting from Corinthians 13, " . . . now we see
   through a glass dimly, but then face to face . . . " Mr. A. did
   not want to pursue the unanswerable questions of "why"
   and "what if." This freed him from wasted emotional energy
   and frustration. (His daughter's seatbelt had not been fas-
   tened.)

SELF-INFLICTED DEATH

Suicide claims the lives of 11.9 young people aged 15 to 24 per
100,000 population, considerably less than those lost to accidents.
The following case history concerns a 24-year-old girl, the second
of three children. She died of a self-inflicted gunshot wound while
away at a state university located about 200 miles from her home.
Her death occurred in July 1986.

Her father, Mr. B., is a self-employed professional and well
respected in the community. He is an active member in his church
and has served on the board of a church-related college in another

state. Mr. B. was born in a small town in the state where he lives and practices. He is a sensitive person and well regarded by his peers.

Mr. B.'s minister drove him and his wife to the university after they received word of their daughter's death. After they identified the body and arrangements were made, they returned home. The most difficult and painful aspect for Mr. B. was his empathy for his daughter's internal struggle. Mr. B. articulated that the pain and hopelessness that she must have experienced in order to have been brought to the point of suicide was the hardest thing for him to handle. It was most distressing to realize that she was unable to ask for help.

In addition to the pain of knowing how much she must have suffered, Mr. B. also acknowledged the pain of his loss. He expressed this feeling as a "void," and along with the realization that "she's not coming home," he suffered greatly.

Another feeling of pain was the feeling that he had failed as a parent. This included the sentiment that if he had been a better father his daughter would have developed the inner resources to recognize her need for help before her pain became so unbearable that suicide seemed the only way out.

In working through his grief, Mr. B. felt that several things were helpful in facilitating the recovery process:

1. Being a professional person, Mr. B. found a professional counselor to assist him and his wife in their attempt to work through their grief. He felt this was particularly helpful to both of them. He explained that they had initially experienced some conflict about the assignment of "blame." The counselor was able to help them to resolve the stress on their marriage that the improper placement of blame had engendered. Citing rigidity and strict religious training as producing the problem, Mr. B. felt the counseling was quite beneficial.
2. The support and acceptance of friends in and out of the church eased what he termed the "stigma" of suicide. Mr. B. stated that they were not treated as "outcasts." This kind of support was appreciated and made him feel less isolated and more accepted.
3. Because of his deep religious faith, the church was very important in the grief process. As mentioned above, his pastor accompanied them on their painful journey to the hospital and advised an "open casket" in the memorial service.

Mr. B. was not certain this was helpful to him but was told
it would be helpful to his daughter's friends. Specifically
Mr. B. mentioned God's wisdom, love and compassion as
being very real to him. Though he could not understand this
tragedy, he was able to trust and this was, perhaps, the
greatest source of strength for him.

4. Being a self-employed person, Mr. B. was able to arrange his
   work schedule so that he came back to his office in about a
   week. He felt that "getting on with life" was therapeutic for
   him.

5. Another avenue of help was using the program of the local
   suicide survivors' support group. Again realizing he was not
   alone or isolated was an affirming experience for Mr. B.

CANCER DEATH

Cancer claims the lives of 5.6 young people aged 15 to 24 per
100,000 population. This young man was unmarried and living at
home. He was 25 years old and had been diagnosed as having
cancer less than 6 months before his death in the oncology ward of
a local hospital. He worked at his job until he became incapaci-
tated about 3 months before he died. He was the youngest of three
children and died in September 1987.

His father, Mr. C., is employed as a civilian security officer at
a military base, and is a military veteran himself. Mr. C. worked
hard to provide for his family and felt that he was financially better
off than when he and his wife were first married. He endeavored to
give his boy "a good home." Most of the details of this interview
were supplied by his wife, since it was still painful for Mr. C. to talk
about his son's death.

Although the onset of the illness was relatively sudden, the
course of his son's illness was erratic. There were times when lab
tests indicated distinct improvement in his condition, then there
were other times when the tests would signal definite deterioration
in his health. This kind of emotional roller coaster was very difficult for the entire family. One minute, hopes would be raised, and
in the next, dashed to pieces.

Soon it became apparent to Mr. C. that his son would not
survive. This increased the stress for Mr. C., who felt great pain in
knowing of the physical discomfort his son was having. This led to
an increasing anger at God. Though not intensely religious, Mr. C.
did feel that "it wasn't fair" that his son suffer so much. His son was
a "good boy and didn't sass his father or mother or come home

drunk." Knowing that his son would never come home again was extremely painful.

Even today the boy's weight-lifting equipment remains in the garage. Mr. C. still finds it difficult to go shopping in a hardware or sporting goods store because it reminds him of things he would like to buy for his son and intensifies the pain of his loss. Although the wound is still open, there are several things that have helped ease the pain and discomfort of his son's death. The following have been Mr. C.'s means of coping with his grief:

1. For Mr. C. it has not been possible to join any support group; his son's death is still too painful to discuss. However, reading books on grief and bereavement has been helpful. Of particular help is *When Bad Things Happen to Good People.*

2. Mr. C.'s wife is a source of great help, and the loss has drawn them even closer. Their mutual support has been one of his major coping mechanisms, though they are not able to "sit still for 5 minutes" at home and have to be "doing something" at all times.

3. Mr. C.'s extended family is also of great assistance. Spending the Christmas and Thanksgiving holidays at the homes of his other children was necessary in the first year after his son's death. Not having to be home by himself on special days eases the sense of loss and loneliness that he might otherwise feel.

4. Mr. C. found it beneficial to return to work immediately so he wouldn't be alone in the house. In addition to the time he spends on the job, he works out at a gym and also practices karate. "Keeping busy" is the main way he copes with his grief.

5. Although his wife goes to the cemetery daily, Mr. C. goes only occasionally. Prior to his accident, Mr. C.'s son had purchased a new car, but even after 6 months, Mr. C. was hardly able to touch the car. Now keeping the car washed and vacuumed gives him a sense of continuity with his son. Mr. C. is now able to drive the car once a week "to keep the battery charged."

AIDS DEATH

Of all the deaths attributed to AIDS (acquired immune deficiency syndrome), 21 percent are in the 20 to 29 age group. Thus, more

than one out of five AIDS deaths are in this category. The young
man in the following case history was 27 years old when he died.
He died of complications of the HIV virus in September 1986. He
had the double risk factors of being a sexually active gay man and
a drug abuser. The contents of this interview were derived from his
AIDS counselor.

This older child was the product of a dysfunctional family; his
natural mother and father had divorced and both had remarried.
His natural mother had virtually nothing to do with her son. However, his father, Mr. D., a retired military officer, did try to maintain contact with his son after the boy left home. The young man,
living in a different state, called his father and told him he was sick
and needed help.

Though the boy was diagnosed as having AIDS in a different
state, he wanted to go to his father's home and get medical attention there. His desire to be cared for by his father created a real
conflict for Mr. D., who loved his son but was fearful of what
business associates, church friends and others might think if he
told them that his son had AIDS.

In the meantime the boy boarded a plane to come home, but he
became so ill during the flight he couldn't continue his journey
home. He was admitted to the hospital in the city where he was to
have changed planes. In the hospital he was given emotional support by a friend. He was never able to get to his father's hometown.
He died in the hospital a month later. By the time Mr. D. arranged
to come to the hospital, the young man had slipped into a coma and
Mr. D. was not able to communicate with his son ever again.

The immense, profound guilt that Mr. D. and other family
members experienced was the most difficult aspect of the grieving
process. His guilt was twofold: not caring for his own son when the
boy really needed him and guilt because the son was gay.

Coping with grief was a difficult and prolonged process for Mr.
D., but there were several things that did seem to be helpful to him:

1. The dying young man received emotional support from a
   gay friend and support arranged by the state's office of
   AIDS services. Mr. D. acknowledged that knowing that his
   son was cared for in the hospital was of some comfort to
   him. Though feeling guilty that he had not personally given
   that care and empathy, Mr. D. was thankful that his son
   received the necessary help from someone. It was a comfort
   to him that his son did not have to suffer alone.

2. Help was given to Mr. D. in a more direct way by a volunteer assigned by the AIDS services office. This volunteer counselor was a woman who was a minister of a local church. In a non-judgmental, objective way she was able to help Mr. D. sort out and understand his feelings.

SUMMARY

Four case histories have been presented as brief vignettes of the grief experienced by fathers of children who died in their twenties. No effort has been made to compare or evaluate the coping mechanisms employed by these four different men. Each person's situation, and the circumstances of the deaths each man experienced, is unique—except for the fact that they were all fathers of the victims. It is readily apparent that fathers, like mothers and siblings, need help in working through the grief process.

In a culture where being masculine sometimes seems to imply the need for emotional concealment or callousness, it is important for those in the helping professions not to assume that grieving is in any way easier for fathers. In fact, since women seem more likely to express their emotions than men, it may be possible that fathers need special help in the grieving process. Unfortunately, this need is not always recognized and, as such, is frequently a need that goes unfulfilled. It is hoped that fathers who lose a child, such as the men described above, will receive the caring attention they so desperately need in their time of grief.

V

The Role of the School

17

Dancing with Feelings:
An Adventure in Storytelling

Donna O'Toole, MA

The story, "Aarvy Aardvark Learns to Play Again" (a read-aloud story for "children of all ages"), is about loss, friendship and hope. It was written as an outgrowth of my own childhood and adult experiences of loss and grief and is meant to help others get in touch with their own feelings of grief. Participants in this grief-release process are encouraged to express and "befriend" their feelings about the story and their personal experiences of loss. The expression of experiences may be demonstrated by talking to the others in the group, telling a story of their own, and even drawing or dancing.

This story has been used with school-age children and their parents in grief counseling and educational settings. It was part of the training of teachers for the North Carolina Children and Grief Project, as well as the Michigan Hospice bereavement coordinators at their "Bridging the Bereavement Gap" statewide conference. The premise is that each person is an "artist" and that our lives are our "art-i-facts." Therefore, participants in this workshop can be teachers as well as students.

The following quotes can be used as meditations and "mirrors" through which the "child within" each of us can understand the theoretical basis for this workshop:

> Grief is not mastered by ceasing to care for the dead, but by abstracting what was fundamentally important in the relationship and rehabilitating it.
>
> —Peter Marris, *Loss and Change*

When we are not allowed to remember, to express our feelings and to grieve or mourn our losses or traumas, whether real or threatened, through the free expression of our child within, we become ill.
— Charles Whitfield, *Healing the Child Within*

Everything is story. Break the pattern that connects and you destroy all quality. Restore the pattern that connects and you enter into all kinds of evolutionary options.

— Jean Houston

While we can listen to the stories of others, and they can listen to ours, perhaps the most healing feature is that We, the storyteller, get to hear our own story.

— Charles Whitfield

Let go of the pain of the past and tell stories to help you reclaim the good. Allow yourself to talk out loud to whomever or whatever you have lost. Regain yourself, freedom to live again.
— Alla Bozarth Campbell, *Life Is Goodbye, Life Is Hello*

An ungrieved loss remains forever alive in our unconscious, which has no sense of time.
— B. G. Simos, *A Time to Grieve: Loss as a Universal Expression*

To find a safe journey through grief to growth does not mean one should forget the past. It means that on the journey we will need safe pathways so that remembrance, which may be pain-full, is possible.
— Donna O'Toole, *Aarvy Aardvark Finds Hope*

Mourning does not achieve the goal of separating the mourner, as if by a river of forgetfulness, from the company of the dead . . . both mourning and life review make use of recurring reminiscences to manifest and affirm the experience of continuity.
— Marc Kaminsky, *The Uses of Reminiscence*

For a relationship remembered is revitalized, brought to life . . . Then giving and receiving become one.
— Robert Johnson, *Ecstasy*

"Lots of animals don't trust their feelings, or they're scared of them," Ralphy had said. But I think feelings are a gift. They are friends that can help us. And they're always there—because they live right inside us. They might be painful or shake us up at times, but, if we listen to them, they will tell us what we need so we can heal and grow.
— Donna O'Toole, *Aarvy Aardvark Finds Hope*

Taking time with our feelings is essential to our growth and happiness. The way out of a painful feeling is through it.
— Charles Whitfield, *Healing the Child Within*

You can't have it without the sun, you can't have it without the rain, Oh the sunshine and the rain, the laughter and the pain, together they make rainbows.
— Matt Schmidt, age 21 (6 months before his death from a chronic terminal illness)

WHITFIELD'S UNITY VS. SEPARATION CYCLES

Unity Cycle

Loss is a part of life and change and will happen for all, even as the seasons change for renewal and continuity. Healing and growth through grief are possible. Unity = an integrated/liberated self:

- Accept feelings
- Trust self
- Express and abstract meaning from, reformulate and transform experiences into a whole
- Intimacy/connectedness/community
- Contentment
- Transformational orientation

Separation Cycle

Losses are not recognized or validated. They are too painful to bear. The importance of losses is minimized, denied or clung to as a way to avoid pain. Separation = the disowned/dependent self:

- Don't feel (numbing)
- Don't talk (don't tell)
- Don't trust (yourself or others)
- Guarded/closed
- Loneliness/isolation/emptiness
- Survival orientation
- Victim/martyr orientation

What Children Need for Unity

1. Recognition of the loss
2. Understanding what the loss means
3. Opportunities to experience the loss
4. Opportunities to discover the meaning of the loss in their life (telling their stories, creative expression, validation)
5. Safety
6. Opportunities to validate the importance of the loss (commemoration and rituals of remembrance)
7. Opportunities to revisit the past to abstract new meanings and to validate the cycles of life

Personal Qualities that Promote Grief that Heals and Revitalizes

1. Trust (self and others)
2. Imagination
3. Curiosity
4. Hope

18

A Model for Grief Intervention and Death Education in the Public Schools

Darcie Sims

Now I lay me down to sleep
I pray the Lord my soul to keep
If I should die before I wake
I pray the Lord my soul to take

This universal child's prayer is meant to give comfort. It may, on the other hand, inspire fear and uncertainty. Although many parents refuse to acknowledge a child's fears and concerns about death, they may religiously sponsor utterance of the words of this prayer each night. Is this the only introduction for children to death? Indeed, for many, it is the sum total of a family's communications about death, loss and grief.

Most children will experience the loss of a pet, friend, relative or neighbor sometime during their school years. By the time you were 5, you knew that squashed bugs made Mom sick, that belly-up goldfish got "flushed" and that everyone seemed to whisper when someone died.

One out of every two children will face the death of a parent or step-parent during their childhood. They will also experience loss from a wide variety of situations, including death, divorce, illness, injury, moves, athletic events or severed relationships. Every child will experience the death of someone or something they love. Yet children are often shuttled off or ignored by adults who may be grieving themselves and not have the energy, resources or under-standing necessary to help. Society tends to pacify itself with the rationale that "children are resilient" and thus fails to recognize that children need as much compassion and concerned support as adults require in adapting to dramatic or traumatic changes in their lives.

Children have an awareness of death even if they don't talk about it. TV, comics, books, conversations overheard and cartoons all help kids form ideas. Death, therefore, becomes a part of a child's experience and should be acknowledged and discussed as naturally as other occurrences. Death—whether caused by acci-dent, illness, murder or suicide—challenges the communication skills of both children and adults. Adults who are dealing with their own sense of loss may find it difficult to respond to children's needs and questions.

When the early experiences of life are wisely handled, they help build sound understandings that make life secure. We cannot deny death, nor can we deny our children the right to experience both the pain and mellowness that death brings. To deny death is to deny that life exists. Yet many of our children do not have a resource of compassionate understanding that allows them to explore and express their ideas, feelings and fears about death. Many adults are simply not comfortable discussing death with children. This chapter has been proposed and implemented be-cause of this lack of support for children experiencing the loss of a loved one. It is designed to address the need for death/loss educa-tion and bereavement support in the public schools.

Teachers, counselors and classmates make up a child's "second family." They, too, have strong feelings when a "family member" experiences grief. For the child touched by loss, the results can be manifested in poor classroom performance, disci-plinary problems, illness and increased absenteeism.

This is an internal program as opposed to an external program contracted by the schools. It was implemented by one staff mem-ber in the 6,000-student school system in Albuquerque, New Mex-ico, between 1986 and 1988. It is based on an empowerment model of program development and implementation. This context en-ables complete maximization of available time and existing re-sources, and also creates a "corps" of trained staff within the school system.

Everyone who has contact with a child can help a child learn to cope with loss. This program becomes the frontline of defense for coping with change and loss within a large public school system.

If we accept the philosophy that grief is a natural and normal reaction to loss of any kind, then loss education and grief management techniques and tools should become an integral part of the students' curriculum. One should not have to wait until a dramatic or traumatic life event occurs to begin preparation for life's crises. Loss education and grief education are linked together.

PROGRAM COMPONENTS

Training and Education

1. Staff training and awareness of personal concepts of loss
2. Training of children's developmental concepts of death
3. Support group facilitation training
4. Community education of adaptation to loss
5. How to utilize loss education programs within classrooms
6. How to develop loss education programs
7. Crisis team development and training

Intervention

1. Direct services to identified children (by school specialist or contracted services)
2. Crisis support teams in each school (staff self-selected)
3. Grief support groups within each school
4. Loss groups and family changes groups
5. "Who am I now?" groups and adaptation to change groups
6. Consultation with staff, parents and community personnel

Resource Services

1. Teaching materials development
2. Curriculum development for loss education (grades K-12)
3. Resource center for school system media development

Many resources are currently available for utilization within the classroom. However, most staffs develop their own once they are convinced they really do have the necessary skills and they feel supported and encouraged in their efforts. A great deal of staff support is required so that they will feel empowered to utilize their own natural creativity and energy to explore with their students the process of adapting to change.

The tools and skills for living with uncertainty, living with unanswerable questions, and learning to live in the present are really life skills that should not have to wait for inclusion in the curriculum until a death has occurred. If we could begin to teach our children (and ourselves) how to live with uncertainty and mystery and unfairness, we would go a long way toward helping our children (and ourselves) learn to cope with whatever life hands us. It is not so much death education and grief management as it is life education and adaptation to change. Learning to adapt and grieve simultaneously is the key to making a successful adjustment.

TOOLS FOR HELPING THE HURT

The task for those wishing to help children cope with change is not to attempt to eliminate stressful events or to protect them, but rather to provide immediate support and a bank of alternatives that a child may draw upon. The elements essential to helping bereaved/grieving children are given below.

1. Know your own feelings.
2. Know your expectations: What do you expect to give? What do you expect in return? Why are you offering it?
3. Be a good observer.
4. Listen to unspoken as well as verbal language. Listen for themes, cues and feelings.
5. Realize that responses may not be obvious and immediate.
6. Give permission to hurt, grieve and express grief.
7. Continue to expect appropriate behaviors. Temper your expectations with kindness and understanding, but continue to expect function and participation.
8. Change should never be an excuse for misbehavior.
9. Bereaved/grieving children need to establish their current identity. Help them in their search.
10. Be available for continued support.
11. Be open and honest. Create an atmosphere of open acceptance that invites questions and fosters confidence and love.
12. Help a child find a supportive peer group. Kids sharing with kids often works wonders.
13. Don't rush through the "stages." Keep in check your impulse to guide the grief process. Each child has a self-regulating time clock for grief.

14. Remember, there are no right or wrong ways to grieve. Some may be less effective than others.

15. Become part of a caring team by establishing communication lines with school, family and community.

16. Maintain discipline. Consistency and an anchor are comforting in a world where everything else is topsy-turvy.

17. Because regressive behavior is common, try to be supportive rather than punitive.

18. Help find constructive outlets for energy, anger and tears.

19. Be guided by the child's needs, not your own.

20. Remember that children and young people will continue to deal with their loss as they grow and mature. The loss will be addressed again and again as they gain new understandings and insights. Continue to be available long after you think they "should be over it."

21. Continue to reach out and care just as you do now. No one lives forever. Nothing lasts or stays the same. All things end at some point. Regardless of how much energy or emotional commitment we invest in a relationship, it cannot last forever. Because one cares, because one invests a certain portion of one's self into the cycles of others, one learns what it is to hurt and to grieve when those cycles are completed in one way or another.

Although painful things do happen in life, it is not "the end of the world" for long. It is not possible nor even desirable to eliminate all stressful life events from the lives of our children. Children learn to cope with loss by moving through the anxiety they feel with the help of supportive adults. As positive experiences in dealing with loss accumulate, we develop the ability to see ourselves as competent, strong, worthwhile individuals and to see life as a challenge we can meet.

Loss hurts, and we cannot find the words to soothe that hurt— there aren't any. We cannot shield our children from the twists and turns of living. We cannot protect them from experiencing life. We can, however, build supports and safety nets, not only for our children, but for ourselves as well. That requires love and faith, strength and support. Hurt and pain have their lessons, and we cannot rob our children of the richness of the tapestry that hurt and love weave together. To eliminate one from the loom is to break the thread and steal away the fabric.

The gifts within love are obvious—we do not dispute them. Yet the gifts within hurt are just as present. We could not understand light if we never knew darkness. "Who am I now?" can become a real challenge rather than a despair if we allow our children and ourselves to claim every experience and support each other as we grow through the triumphs and the trials.

> Now I lay me down to sleep
> I pray the Lord my soul to keep
> To keep me safe all through the night
> To wake me in the morning light

We cannot protect our children from the rain, but we can go together in search of the parade.

19

The Effectiveness of
Death Education

Richard A. Pacholski, PhD

There is a scene in a garden in Shakespeare's play *Twelfth Night* where Orsino, Duke of Illyria, greets Feste the clown with a hale and hearty "How dost thou, my good fellow?" Feste responds like a typical Shakespearean fool—obliquely, unexpectedly, not quite to the point; indeed, we might call his words silly and irrelevant, until we remember that Shakespeare's fools are typically his wisest characters.

How dost thou, my good fellow?

Truly, sir, the better for my foes and the worse for my friends.

Just the contrary: the better for thy friends.

No, sir, the worse.

How can that be?

Marry, sir, they praise me and make an ass of me. Now, my foes tell me plainly that I am an ass; so that by my foes, sir, I profit in the knowledge of myself, and by my friends I am abused. . . .

As death educators we should spend some time meditating upon this: there may be some truth in our foes' assertions that we are asses. For the sake of fairness, and in order to take a look at the other side, I now yield the floor to those who disagree with us, in other words, the people and groups who are vehemently against educating children about death in school, and invite them to make their case.

The first person I would like to "take on" is Phyllis Schlafly (M.A., Harvard; J.D., Washington University), listed since 1977 as one of *Good Housekeeping* magazine's ten most admired women in the world. Mrs. Schlafly is president of the Eagle Forum, a national pro-family organization. Not long ago *Death and Life*, the newsletter of the thanatology program at Brooklyn College, reported on an article written by Mrs. Schlafly, appearing in the *Brooklyn Spectator*, in which she calls into question the attempts of schools to include curricula on suicide, death, dying and euthanasia (Bowlby, personal communication).

> If you assume that suicide courses would tell teenagers that suicide is wrong, unhealthy, socially irresponsible and a mistake, you are living in a dream world about public education today. More probably suicide courses would tell teenagers that suicide is a matter of personal choice and that lots of people do it, including famous people. . . . What we are witnessing is an attempt by unlicensed psychologists (teachers, counselors, guidance people, social workers) to conduct group therapy in the classroom. They have no professional credentials for this, and they are dealing with a psychological dimension in which anything they do is apt to be far worse than nothing at all.

Schlafly insists that the schools should solicit prior parental consent before offering courses on suicide and death and dying (which Schlafly equates to psychological tests or treatment).

In 1984, in congressional hearings on the Hatch Amendment, testimony was taken from amendment supporters. Schlafly has cited much of it in her book, *Child Abuse in the Classroom*, distributed widely in conservative circles. In arguing for passage of the amendment (which was to provide that parents must give consent to death education and related educational programs), one parent objected to a classroom showing of the film version of Shirley Jackson's short story, *The Lottery*, and after recounting the gory details of the story, claimed that "No one understood the film or the reason for showing it" (p. 153). Another parent objected to the Ombudsman Drug Education curriculum as emphasizing affective response rather than information or facts about drugs. Beginning from the premise that there are no right or wrong answers, students discuss statements and situations like these:

> it's OK to try anything once; a drug dealer is just a business person like anyone else; and, it's impossible to become an alcoholic just by drinking beer. . . . Do you think it's all right to lie, cheat, steal, break laws once in a while, or only at certain times? Why is the choice of 'never' never given? . . . [Then] the class plays a survival game and decides which three people to eliminate from the group. This frightening strategy desensitizes children to the worth and dignity of human life. . . . Where does that leave the sick, the elderly, the

retarded, or the handicapped persons? . . . Finally, in this drug curriculum . . . we find exercises in death education. The children write their own epitaph or obituaries. This also desensitizes children to any uncomfortable feelings that they may have about death and dying. . . . (Schlafly, pp. 402–403).

Another parent notes of the survival game that it destroys religious beliefs, for the clergyman is always the oldest, and thus is certain to be eliminated. Still another parent objects to the design of certain questionnaires:

When my daughter was 12 years old . . . she was asked: 'What reasons would motivate you to commit suicide?' Five reasons were listed from which she was expected to choose. She was given a list of ten ways of dying, including violent death, and asked to list them in order of 'most to least preferred.' She was asked what should be done to her if she was terminally ill. Two of the five choices offered by the framers of this questionnaire involved forms of mercy killing. . . . The ways we would teach our children to deal with terminal illness were completely left out of the choices presented to our daughter. The authors built their values into the answers, but conveniently left our values out. . . . What they in fact do is to tell children what to think. This is indoctrination and manipulation of young minds of the most hideous sort (Schlafly, pp. 371–372).

One mother reported that her son, having recently lost his father, was taken on a field trip with his class to the embalming room of the local funeral parlor.

The most vocal opponents of death education in the schools have spoken out against nuclear weapons, nuclear war and peace studies programs as well. Schlafly (1985) calls the five major curricula in nuclear war currently in use

psychological treatment courses which produce guilt, fear and despair. The nuclear war courses invade the pupils' privacy about political affiliations and attitudes, and attempt to change the students' attitudes to conform to the authors' prejudices and politics. . . . [It] is so sad that school children are deliberately taught to be afraid and are trained to feel helpless and overwhelmed. Children should be given hope, idealism and faith in the future (pp. 410–413).

Another of our foes, Dr. Herb London, a dean at New York University and author of the book *Why are They Lying to Our Children?* objects to what he sees in the schools as a heavy emphasis on hazards and problems, a "variety of options and scenarios of despair," and a concomitant subordination of promise and hope. Another critic, Barbara Morris, in her book, *Change Agents in the*

Schools, speaks for many death education opponents when she complains about the morose reading assignments, the questionnaires probing student attitudes and the field trips to cemeteries, mortuaries and crematories which, she concludes, serve only to promote secular humanism (Bowlby, personal communication).

Finally, we need to acknowledge Mel and Norma Gabler of Longview, Texas, who have attained prominence recently for their wholesale attacks on all manner of sin, moral relativism and godless humanism in a whole range of school textbooks and curricula. In various of their printed materials distributed widely in conservative circles, the Gablers argue that humanistic values constitute a religion bent on setting itself up in place of Christianity. The Gablers have scored death education as fostering principles of the "Humanist Manifesto" and thus violating Biblical truth. They focus on snippets like these from high school health or home economics texts:

> Dying is an orgasmic event.... The thought of death sometimes occurs in a sexual context ... in that the event of orgasm, like the event of dying, involves a surrender to the involuntary and the unknown.... [In] the experience of dying, the individual experiences a cosmic consciousness, characterized by a sense of unity with other people, nature and the universe; a feeling of being outside time and space; and extraordinary feelings of contentment and ecstasy.

Thus, for the Gablers, death educators are teaching that repulsiveness is beautiful and that destruction of the body unites individuals with all of humanity. Such tenets and goals of death education violate Biblical principles: for example, from Acts: "There shall be a Resurrection of the dead, both of the just and the unjust," and from Proverbs: "He that sinneth against Me wrongeth his own soul: all they that hate me love death." The Gablers object that

> the humanistic architects of death education never present the Christian hope of life after death. They give the students the depressing pagan doctrine that this life is all there is and death ends everything.... We all recognize that death is part of life and must be dealt with, but ... it is cruel to dwell on death education or teach it without benefit of any expressed belief in God, the hereafter or the resurrection (Bowlby, personal communication).

Of course it would be easy to dismiss these people as yahoos, anti-intellectuals, intolerant rednecks, right-wing kooks and Bible-thumpers. It is clear that in the case of Schlafly's organization, Eagle Forum, these people have a narrowly focused, well-financed political agenda. It is clear that like any advocate, ourselves included, these people are not always above manipulating evidence, whether statistics or anecdotal testimony or quoted passages from enemies or supporters alike, to bolster their own cases. But in the foregoing litany of objections to death education, regardless of the motives or the objectivity of the critics, we as death educators may see ourselves writ large as fools:

- if we stop short of labeling suicide as wrong, as a mistake, as evil;
- if, in using a piece of literature in the classroom, we fail to do a thorough literary analysis—of symbol, theme, irony, ambiguity and the like;
- if we show a film like "The Lottery" and let it go at that;
- if, in role-playing or game-playing (like "Who Survives?" for example), we fail to fully explain contexts and rationale, or if we fail to give voice or hearing to a full range of opinion and belief;
- if we continue as teachers (no matter the subject or level) to depend on multiple choice (multiple guess), fill-in-the-blank, true-false or other simplistic testing instruments, particularly with subject matter or in situations inappropriate for them;
- if we do any sort of death education activity without a well-founded knowledge of our pupils, or without making certain that, with troubling subject matter or activities, pupils always have an out, or at least that students are made confident that we as teachers are available for help or for listening, that we care;
- if, in dealing with nuclear issues, we ignore the political dimension;
- if, in dealing with euthanasia or suicide, we ignore the legal, moral and ethical dimensions, including the denominational religious dimensions;
- if we fail to assert, to stress, to convey emphatically the life-affirming nature of death education.

We may indeed be writ large as fools if we ignore or even pussyfoot around the Christian, the Buddhist, the Jewish, or the whole host of other religious answers to thanatological questions, answers as meaningful and as valid as any others we've come up with, whether we personally believe them or not, answers devoutly held by many members of our school communities and constituencies, answers fully worth respect and attention, even if personally we are John Dewey humanists or doubters, no matter if we have fallen away from, or risen above or beyond the faith of our fathers.

A somewhat more reasoned critique of death education appeared in the February 1988 issue of *The Atlantic:* "Mortal Fears: Courses in Death Education Get Mixed Reviews," by Fergus M. Bordewich. It seems to me that this ostensibly thoughtful critic devotes an undue amount of time to the sorts of anecdotal horror stories I've just reviewed. His somewhat fuzzy metaphor over-states: "The canopy of death education clearly shelters a jungle of idiosyncratic and sometimes highly questionable practices" (p. 31)—practices, by the way, collected and publicized in the last 5 years—and probably fed to Bordewich—by people like Schlafly and the Gablers. But Bordewich goes on to recapitulate what many of us have recognized and lamented for years. First, there is no standard curriculum for death education in grades K to 12 or any part thereof; where death education is taught it is typically taught in units or on call, whether on an ad hoc basis by a teacher who happens to be interested or is just returned from a week-end workshop, or because a need, occasion or question has arisen, or because there may be a section on a death education issue in the health or science or literature text. Second, since there is no standard curriculum, there are no universally acknowledged cur-ricular standards—not for content, not for methodology. Thus, Bordewich insists that "no one can reliably gauge the effect that 'mind games' and death-focused exercises have on psychologically fragile young people, on those who have recently experienced a parent's or a friend's death, or on those who are involved with drugs" (p. 32).

There are no standard curricula, no curricular standards, and no standard teachers either. As we know, credentialing in death education is not required. I understand that in the United States not one college or university department of education that creden-tials teachers either offers or requires any course in death studies. Thus, would-be teachers may or may not have picked up some death education on their own in college. They may or may not go to workshops, in-services or conventions of appropriate organiza-tions. Teachers of death education are generally self-taught, what-ever that may mean. Only a few teachers in North America are members of the Association for Death Education and Counsel-ing (a 1985 count identified fewer than two dozen); only a handful have successfully passed through the Association's certification program.

We have been into "death and dying" for some 20 years now, considering the 1969 Kübler-Ross book as the *locus classicus*. But we don't even know how much death education is being done in the schools today—how many courses, how many units, how many teachers. Hannelore Wass has estimated that no more than 5% of elementary teachers handle death education in any planned way. At the secondary level, a recent survey in New York state suggested that 14% of health educators teach a unit on death; another 64% of health educators surveyed incorporate death education in units on other subjects. Other than such spotty reports we just don't know. How many public and private K-12 schools are there in North America? Between 90,000 and 100,000? And how many school students are there? Upwards of 50 million?

Mel Gabler and Phyllis Schlafly have done microscopic analyses of the many health and home economics textbooks that provide some coverage of death education topics; they have studied as well the death-oriented sampling of short stories and poems in a number of literature texts. By their lights, of course, their analyses yielded only dirt—which they are now blowing throughout the land. Have we looked at those books, we as death education leaders in our home communities and schools? What have we done as professionals—as teachers and scholars—to critically evaluate the work of our peers? Are we familiar with the textbooks of our colleagues in other departments? Do we know what our professional associations are doing—if anything—in the name of death studies?

Leaders in the death studies field, like Darrell Crase, were warning us in 1978 about the need to assess the impact of death education:

> Thanatologists are going to be held more accountable for their actions and for the efficacy of death education. At present this isn't being done.... Anyone ... can become an expert overnight. The accountability model will eventually curtail this practice.... Professional organizations will also need to assume a partnership role in the accountability process. Behavioral and attitudinal objectives must be articulated at the front end of the instructional process.... Once these objectives are established we must more fully utilize reliable and sophisticated assessment/research techniques to guide us in this adventure (pp. 429–430).

It's now more than 10 years later in our adventure, and we've got the right wing dumping on us and thoughtful critics questioning our professional behavior and qualifications, if not our basic intelligence. More than a few of our number, doing stupid things, are making all of us look bad.

All this is not to say that we good guys have been doing nothing all this time. Let me speak first about the key professional association in this field, the Association for Death Education and Counseling. Membership in the Association is up and growing. Coming off several very successful annual conferences, the Association is now financially able to undertake major new research and other projects. For example, the Association's certification program is now being significantly upgraded. In 1988 a large class of applicants took the newly designed certification course in Orlando, Florida. A commission appointed at the 1988 convention, including such people as Hannelore Wass, Darrell Crase and Gordon Thornton, has begun a formal survey of death education programs and activities in the schools preparatory to its working to develop standards and to design the model curricula we have all been waiting for. I would urge everyone working in any way in death education or death-related counseling to join the Association. Now that the Association is being handled by an experienced, professional management firm it is offering improved services to members at a time when, with major new funding, the leadership of the organization is spearheading important research efforts.

Despite detractors' claims and our own sense of potential still unfulfilled, effective death education has been defined, outlined and refined. We know how to describe effective death education teachers. We know how to design curricula. We have verbalized eloquently what death education can do and how badly it is needed at this time in our history. For example, Charles Corr has described and defined the effective teacher of death education in his book, done with Hannelore Wass, *Helping Children Cope with Death* (1982). Corr emphasizes the responsibility of teachers and would-be teachers to prepare themselves, emotionally and professionally, for the task. He offers guidelines for identifying the real needs of children at various developmental levels, for actively listening to and effectively communicating with children, and for cooperating with the various school-related constituencies—parents, teachers, counselors, administration, clergy people and other caregivers—in developing and implementing effective death education programs. "No one has a corner on wisdom about death," says Corr. Building on Gene Knott's classic outline of the goals of death education, Corr explains the basic goals for helpers which must undergird any such program. Then he outlines model teacher-training programs, both formal and self-study, and identifies resources, including books, bibliographies, periodicals, audiovisual media and organizations.

Teachers of middle and high school students should know the book by Charles Corr and Joan McNeil entitled *Adolescence and Death* (1986). One of its 17 richly informative chapters, "Death Education: Developing a Course of Study for Adolescents," by Nina Rosenthal, describes the effective death education program as promising three major outcomes: (1) the sharing of information, involving chiefly the cognitive domain, with which students can then develop accurate concepts, make decisions and take positive action; (2) the development of self-awareness and of healthy attitudes toward death and dying content, topics and issues; this outcome, in other words, helps children to understand their personal reactions to information presented, encourages them to listen actively to the expressed reactions of others, and then fosters free discussion and sharing of one's own concerns and opinions and those of others; and (3) the fostering of behaviors aimed at helping both oneself and others; this development of helping skills involves acquiring a tolerance for varying points of view and an understanding of emotionally laden language, and the development of good communication skills. Analyzing each of these three outcomes in depth, Rosenthal explores instructional objectives, class content and resources, and suggests methodology and techniques of evaluation. Like all the recent books, articles and chapters mentioned here, Rosenthal's study is most helpful in its presentation of reference material, all of it required reading for anyone who would call herself or himself a death educator.

One other basic sourcebook is *Childhood and Death*, edited by Wass and Corr (1984). Three chapters discuss effective death education, offering guidance to parents and teachers. First, Joan McNeil advises parents about death education in the home. Second, Ute Carson shows teachers at the preschool and elementary levels how to be alert for and use effectively those teachable moments in the classroom occasioned by small deaths: whether separation from pets or toys or people, or the actual deaths of classroom pets or plants, playground birds or neighborhood animals. Carson analyzes as well the instructional opportunities inherent in fairy tales and other imaginative literature regularly read and discussed in school classrooms.

Finally, in a remarkably well organized and thorough chapter nicely recapping recent scholarship, "Death Education in the Schools for Older Children," Dixie and Darrell Crase discuss teacher competencies and do an especially helpful and informative analysis of the characteristics of pre-adolescent and adolescent development with which death educators must be familiar. The section of their chapter on curriculum surveys goals for death education, identifies major published curriculum guides and addresses problems of evaluation. The concluding research and assessment section verbalizes well what responsible death educators know needs to be done in terms of addressing the real effectiveness of death education programs on the healthy development of children's attitudes. We must have answers to such questions as these:

> Why death education? What lasting effect does it have on student behavior? When should it begin and end? . . . What are the behavioral and attitudinal changes desired? . . . We now need to move from an essentially cosmetic approach . . . to a more structured model that is supported by research. Death education is important; it can meet several objectives aimed at improving the quality of life. . . . But to be valued and accepted by society as a lasting, meaningful, and impactful educative process considerable work needs to be done within the assessment/research sphere (p. 360).

I will conclude with some personal observations. I am not nearly as concerned about the resistance to our work of the Gablers, the Schlaflys and the Bordewichs of the world as I am about some simple factual realities about our schools and school systems. It's not that parents and PTAs, school boards, administrators and teachers are opposed to death education; surveys have shown that even parents of preschoolers, as long as they understand the goals and methods of thanatological instruction, in general support it. It's not that college and university education departments aren't convinced of its value. But with a dozen similarly noble subjects, activities, local interests, problems and concerns clamoring for inclusion in an already overcrowded school curriculum, we're not apt to be very successful in our efforts, at least not soon. This seems especially so in terms of any free-standing curriculum we might propose. While some few established school disciplines have begun to be involved—health, physical education, home economics and language arts—most other disciplines are not, nor are college and university education departments.

What all this says to me is that those of us in mainstream higher education departments, who are also involved professionally in death studies, have much work to do in converting our own departmental colleagues as well as our peers in other disciplines, particularly education. There may be other ways to proceed—

certainly as death educators we can continue to train, support and encourage individual students and teachers in our classrooms and communities as they encounter and handle thanatological issues; of course we should continue to write and speak to public audiences, to offer and attend more conferences. But let's not expect any revolution in the schools.

My last point is a profession of faith. Death education is worthy of our continuing study and teaching because it is a supremely moral subject. Not to put too fine a point on it, I believe effective death education is religion in action. Death education enables a person to formulate essential moral judgments, operating from basic definitions. Who is my neighbor? What is the nature and worth of the individual? Who are the contemporary equivalents of the Biblical sick, the lame, the halt, the blind, the Samaritans, the lepers? Of course they include the cancer patient, the brain-damaged, the institutionalized aged, the Alzheimer's victim. Death education forces one to take a stand about the responsibilities of human beings for one another. If indeed all men are brothers, and I am my brothers' keeper, then I have responsibilities for my brother dying of AIDS. This, the heart of the lesson, we would teach our children—pre-K, K-12, whatever the level: you are your brothers' and sisters' keepers; you are morally obligated to respond, as well as you may, with love, concern and caregiving to the bereaved, the depressed, the diseased, the dying and the dead.

Building upon such moral judgments, death education, like religion narrowly construed, encourages right thinking: about feelings, about attitudes and about beliefs—about fearing what must be feared, about recognizing ghosts and bogeys for what they are, about distinguishing between imagined and real foes, imagined and real evil, imagined and real sources of harm and injustice. Death education fosters hope for a positive and beneficial outcome, if not in this life then in another or future life, or in another way, or from another point of view. Death education fosters right thinking about faith—faith that human life in all its manifestations, in all its infinite multiplicity and uncertainty, in its symbolic shadowing forth, in its ambiguity and irony, has purpose and is worth living.

On the foundation, then, of sound knowledge and moral attitudes, opinions and beliefs, one accepts the responsibility for moral action. We share the conviction about the great promise of death education in fostering behaviors—"life-genic behaviors," to use Dan Leviton's phrase—on all levels of the human community: individual, familial, societal and global. Thus, for example, moral attitudes result in one's hand touching one's grieving classmate, one's voice insisting on tolerance for the AIDS victim, one's energy given over time to Gramps with Alzheimer's or to the Compassionate Friends. Death education is applied religion—the application of spiritually grounded moral beliefs and attitudes in daily life. The Gablers and Schlaflys are right. If death education is religion in action, it is humanism in action as well—seeing our own human condition in every other human being, thinking not in parochial terms but in global terms, acting not out of selfish, sectarian, local or nationalistic impulse, but out of an ecumenical vision, embracing all who share our human condition.

If death education is thus religious activity in its core, that does not mean that it must be construed as a substitute for denominational religion or that it is to be blamed for usurping the roles of the church or family in inculcating moral and ethical values. Nor am I willing to agree with our foes that death and dying issues should be left to parents or the clergy. I am a parent; I've been in a seminary. As well as you, I know the flaws of parents, the real workaday limitations of priests, ministers and rabbis. I know that death studies is the business of scholars and teachers. We know as well that we have got to get our classrooms and our study tables in order. Death education can be an important means of supplementing the efforts of all thinking parents, teachers, counselors, clergy and caregivers as we work to raise our children well and to provide for them a healthy present and a more secure future.

REFERENCES

Bordewich, Fergus M. Mortal fears: courses in death education get mixed reviews. *The Atlantic*, February 1988, pp. 30–34.

Bowlby, Bonnie. Eagle Forum. Personal communication.

Corr, Charles, and Joan McNeil, eds. *Adolescence and Death*. New York: Springer, 1986.

Crase, Darrell. The need to assess the impact of death education. *Death Education* 1(4), 429–430, 1978.

Schlafly, Phyllis, ed. *Child Abuse in the Classroom*. Alton, IL: Pere Marquette Press, 1985.

Wass, Hannelore, et al. *Dying: Facing the Facts*. Washington: Hemisphere, 1979.

Wass, Hannelore, and Charles Corr, eds. *Helping Children Cope with Death*. Washington: Hemisphere, 1982.

———. *Childhood and Death*. Washington: Hemisphere, 1984.

WINTERSPRING
P. O. BOX 8169
MEDFORD, OREGON 97504